By Popular Demand

The Adelaide Festival Centre Story

Adelaide Festival Centre Trust

in association with

Wakefield Press

Box 2266

Kent Town

South Australia 5071

First published 1998

Edited by Penelope Curtin
Designed by design BITE, Adelaide
Typeset by Clinton Ellicott, MoBros, Adelaide
Printed and bound by Hyde Park Press, Adelaide

National Library of Australia
Cataloging-in-publication entry

Campbell, Lance, 1949–   .
By popular demand; the Adelaide Festival
Centre story.

ISBN 1 86254 456 5.

1. Adelaide Festival Centre – History.
2. Adelaide Festival Centre – Pictorial works.
3. Adelaide Festival Centre Trust – History.
4. Centres for the performing arts – South
Australia – Adelaide. I. Title

792.0994231

42nd Street

By Popular Demand

The Adelaide Festival Centre Story

Lance Campbell

ADELAIDE FESTIVAL CENTRE
25TH ANNIVERSARY
1973-1998

"I love this place so much I could sit and watch an empty stage."

PHOTO

A performance in 25 acts

Left: The Space

"A rude Mechanical in the Athens of the South"

Geoffrey Rush

For five and a half fabulous years from the early to mid-eighties, the Adelaide Festival Centre was my professional home. And like any true home they graciously kept a made-up couch for me in the metaphorical sun-room for my frequent return visits during the rest of the decade and into the mid-nineties.

Inspirational news of this complex and George Ogilvie's reign at the Playhouse had already tantalised us up north in the early seventies when I was in residence at the Queensland Theatre Company. In 1981, when I was contracted for two plays back-to-back, the Playhouse was already steeped in vigorous folklore and a welter of traditions. Unlike its interstate cousins whose regimes generally held court for decades or more, the State Theatre Company had kept itself lively with a regular turnover of directorship.

In the wake of Jim Sharman's extraordinary and unforgettable redefinition of the Adelaide Festival in 1982, I enthusiastically became a member of his Lighthouse Company for two years, and then artistic director of Magpie Theatre for Young People for another two. I felt wholeheartedly that I truly belonged to a building and a company that had no rival anywhere on the continent.

It was a personal Golden Age for me. Like Shakespeare's happy few at the Rose or the Globe, I dreamily treasured that I was a rude Mechanical in the Athens of the South.

The Festival Theatre was alive with great shows and great audiences – beautiful opportunities to experience the London Symphony Orchestra and the entire Beethoven Symphonic and Concerto Cycle with Ashkenazy at the keyboard and on the podium; Pina Bausch's *Bluebeard*; all eight hours of *Nicholas Nickleby*. The Bistro was always seething with camaraderie, gossip, a sometimes healthy bewilderment at the nature of programming, and a lack of apathy. Thirsts for art, community and industry were passionately slaked.

I was conscious that our theatre community was an important part of the community of Adelaide and of South Australia. Adelaide people felt strongly about their Festival Centre, and what went on in it.

Perhaps time or memory, or memories of too much time in the Bistro – or even Lark and Tina's or the Austral or the Fezbah – have distorted the . . . ah, the Fezbah! My medieval heroes the Clemencic Consort did a gig there and held a well-oiled audience spellbound with just a tiny pipe and a weird drum. Most of the major comedians and cabaret artists of Australia and beyond honoured its stage.

The Centre has given me a lot of highs. I barnstormed shamelessly and happily on a Glen Finch-constructed set, wielding a John Meyer prop and sporting a Helga Bechler hat. I expanded my ongoing relationship with director Neil Armfield. I faced the baying crowds as host of Theatresports. I pitched Shakespeare in between beauty products on *A Touch of Elegance.* I workshopped *Everyman* with Year 9 students at Thebarton High. I directed several Follies to celebrate ourselves.

Live performers need their breeding grounds and their stamping grounds. The Festival Centre is both these things and has been for 25 exciting years. I am so proud to have been a part of the fervent culture on this particular Adelaide agar dish.

I am sure this vibrant, constantly evolving centre for the arts will continue to flourish for generations of South Australians to come.

Geoffrey Rush

The offer came out of the blue. My agent phoned to say two producers wanted to know whether I was interested in playing Mrs Anna in *The King and I* in Australia. The producers turned out to be the Adelaide Festival Centre Trust and the Gordon/Frost Organisation.

That phone call changed the shape of my life for the next seven years, right up to now. Although at that time I had begun to do more stage work and fewer films, I had only been in one musical before and I wasn't sure about a leading role. But director Chris Renshaw, producer John Frost and the Trust's Tim McFarlane persuaded me. I was also very curious about Australia.

I loved the Festival Theatre from the moment the cast came from rehearsal at Her Majesty's for a first walk on the set. The crew was everywhere and it didn't seem possible the show would be ready on time. The theatre became my home for the next two months, through the technical and dress rehearsals, the previews and the run. The Centre crew and staff couldn't have been more welcoming or more helpful.

We finally opened *The King and I* in the Festival Theatre on 11 June 1991 and the rest is musical theatre history, not only in Australia but in America too. The audiences were wonderful and when I made my entrance to greet the English Ambassador, the applause was always loud. It didn't take me long to realise the reception wasn't for me. It was for my magnificent ballgown, and it came as no surprise to me when our designer Roger Kirk won the best costume Tony on Broadway.

Two years later I returned to the Festival Theatre, playing opposite my sister Juliet in *Fallen Angels*. It is a tribute to the theatre's versatility that it works just as well for the spoken word as it does for a Rodgers and Hammerstein musical.

Since then I've spent another year of my life touring with *The King and I* in the United States. Being part of such a brilliant production from the start has been one of the most satisfying experiences of my career, and my time in Adelaide is a time I cherish.

The Festival Centre develops and encourages artists, and cares about its audiences.

For me it is a very special place full of very special people, for very special people.

Hayley Mills

Now look here Don. I'm running out of friends to invite to perform at the Festival because our venues are inadequate. I can't ask Benjamin Britten to perform Les Illuminations *in Centennial Hall. We're scraping the bottom of the cultural barrel here. You're going to have to plan a proper centre for the Festival.*

– remembered excerpt from a one-way conversation between Sir Robert Helpmann, artistic director of the Adelaide Festival of Arts, and Premier Don Dunstan, late 1967.

Sir Robert Helpmann

First it was to be a Festival Concert Hall overlooking Adelaide. That was in 1965.

In early 1968, after Sir Robert Helpmann's meeting with Don Dunstan, the New York theatre consultant Thomas DeGaetani recommended that South Australia and the City of Adelaide, with assistance from the Commonwealth, undertake the construction of a South Australian Performing Arts Centre.

Later that year the new Premier, Steele Hall, decided a Festival Theatre would be built on the banks of the River Torrens, and earthworks began on the southern edge of Elder Park in March 1970.

Back in office, Dunstan took DeGaetani's advice and adopted Hall's site.

The Adelaide Festival Centre Trust was created by an Act of Parliament.

On Saturday 2 June 1973, the Prime Minister, Gough Whitlam, opened the Adelaide Festival Theatre at a gala performance of Act Two, Scene 1 of Beethoven's opera *Fidelio* and Beethoven's *Choral Symphony*.

Peter Brook's legendary *A Midsummer Night's Dream* bumped in two days later. Then followed the 15th International Adelaide Film Festival, the pianist Vladimir Ashkenazy, the soprano Victoria de los Angeles, the Australian Opera and the Leningrad Kirov Ballet.

Australia's first multi-purpose arts centre was open for show business. The Playhouse, the Space and the Amphitheatre began their public lives little more than a year later. Queen Elizabeth II dedicated the Plaza at the official Centre completion ceremony in March 1977.

The Centre is recognised the world over. For a quarter of a century the great stars and the great shows have played there, and will go on playing there. Throughout its 25 years the Centre has been home to the Adelaide Festival and the base for one of Australia's leading entrepreneurial arts organisations.

Hundreds of thousands of South Australians and their friends from interstate and overseas use the many forms of the Festival Centre every year. It is the cultural centrepiece of a city, its arts and entertainment energy centre, the focus of its creative future.

Opposite: 2 June 1973 – Beethoven's *Choral Symphony*

By popular demand, this is the Festival Centre story.

CHAPTER 1

"They said it couldn't be done!"

Gough Whitlam commanded the stage like a latter-day Roman Emperor. The 2000 of his subjects arranged before him could rest assured they were sitting in "this building, this magnificent achievement".

Don Dunstan was triumphant in his polo-necked evening shirt: "They said it couldn't be done anywhere, but we've done it!"

Anthony Steel was a nervous wreck. That day he had cleaned the theatre with his bare hands, speck by speck.

Two Trustees were stuck in the lift.

Sir Mark Oliphant had to wait in an office. Protocol demanded that the Governor of South Australia absent himself when someone less vice-regal than himself was stealing the show. The latter-day Roman Emperor was doing the honours.

Outside, the rain made rivers of mud on the construction site. Inside, euphoria reigned.

Shortly after 8 pm on the night of Saturday 2 June 1973, the Prime Minister of Australia opened the Festival Theatre before a black-tie audience of Adelaide society and show business guests from the east. The Festival Theatre "will be a source of great pride to the people of South Australia and the City of Adelaide", Whitlam said.

"It will also, I believe, be an inspiration to the whole of Australia."

Then on with the show, the gala opening performance.

Composer and Trustee Richard Meale wrote a fanfare. The trumpeters and drummers of the Central Command Band played it.

Act Two, Scene One of Beethoven's only opera, *Fidelio*, filled the first half of the program. Australian Opera singers Ronald Dowd, Neil Warren-Smith, Rosemary Gordon, Raymond Myers and Lyn Clayton, with conductor Georg Tintner, provided the first of the Theatre's multiple choices.

After an extended interval in which the bubbles flowed in the foyers,

Gough Whitlam – "an inspiration to the whole of Australia"

Nerves of Steel

Several hours before the opening, theatre consultant Tom Brown could see Anthony Steel was in a state. "What are you going to be eating this evening?" he asked. "I'll meet you here with something at 6.30." Brown brought sandwiches and French champagne to the general manager's office. The tears subsided. Today Steel says, "Nervous? Me? I never had any doubts. I relished the whole thing".

Strike one

The first scheduled opening of the Festival Theatre, on 3 March 1973, was cancelled because of a building industry strike in December 1972. Sir Robert Helpmann was to have choreographed a moon ballet for the Australian Ballet and danced in *Cinderella* on the night.

conductor Ladislav Slovak and the South Australian Symphony Orchestra stepped on to the stage and into the orchestra shell for Beethoven's *Choral Symphony* with the Adelaide Festival Chorus.

Anthony Steel stepped from the audience into the Chorus. Not only did Adelaide have a lyric theatre; it also had a lyric theatre with a lyric tenor general manager.

At the close of the show, the applause was sustained, exultant. What else would you expect from a captive audience, the largest gathering of prisoners of art in the State's history?

You would expect nothing less than a standing ovation for such a success story.

In a little over three years, Adelaide had beaten Sydney and its Opera House to the punch by four months and, for $6.6 million, at about one-tenth of the cost. Perth had its new Concert Hall and Canberra its mid-size Theatre Centre. The Victorian Arts Centre and the Queensland Performing Arts Centre would have to wait until the next decade.

Here was the first major lyric theatre in the country, purpose-built and fitted out for concerts, opera, dance and musical theatre. And attached to it was the guarantee of more to come – a plaza, a playhouse, an experimental theatre, an amphitheatre, galleries, public art, education and youth programs. The complete cultural centre would soon be at hand in the middle of the city, available to all people and all tastes, and a home for the Adelaide Festival.

But there was more to the night than interstate rivalry and one-upmanship. Adelaide freed itself of provincialism on 2 June 1973. In the Festival Theatre it did not celebrate the exceeding of expectations, as provincials do. It celebrated the magnitude of its achievement.

This was a bloody good theatre – good to look at, good to be in, good for South Australia. It had verve and style. Adelaide had broken from its colonial past. The theatre was modern. It might even become a work of art.

Once it became a political and practical possibility, the Festival Theatre had been created for the people. Two weeks earlier, 40,000 South Australians inspected the theatre in a single day. The queue stretched along King William Road to North Terrace, with a 45-minute wait, and the viewing time was extended by two hours.

In February 1970 a public appeal for a Festival Theatre reached its target amount of $100,000 in a week. The appeal was soon oversubscribed, and an extra $63,000 was set aside for the future building's artworks.

Fidelio graffito

To show off the depth of the Festival Theatre stage, the back wall was exposed during the *Fidelio* half of the opening performance. On the wall was painted LIBERTAD, Spanish for "freedom". Minus the TAD, the word is still visible today. When Gough Whitlam saw it, he said, "If that means LIBERALS I'm going home!"

Below: *Fidelio*, 2 June 1973

"Will you kindly shut your trap about what you jokers did in Adelaide and let us finish this thing"

Sleepy beak

A Supreme Court judge slept in the stalls through the entire *Choral Symphony*. "Not an easy thing to do, quite an heroic performance," says a junior colleague of the time, now himself a judge.

Left: Norm Mitchell in *The News*

Dress sense, musical choices

Within a week of first night, what to wear to the Festival Theatre was a hot topic around town. So also was the opening program. Too late, it was suggested some "sparkling" Paul McCartney compositions would have been more suitable than Beethoven's "stodgy" *Ninth Symphony*. A small start, but arts debate had come out into the open in Adelaide, thanks to its new public facility. Some patrons plumped for evening dress in the face of the "conformity and mediocrity" of jeans and slacks-suits. James Irwin, a former Lord Mayor, took the middle ground in a letter to *The Advertiser* on 12 June 1973. "As far as I am aware," Sir James wrote, "people may wear any decent clothing they wish. If the exhibitionists among us want to wear peculiar outfits, let them do so. Those who prefer the relative anonymity, and for me greater comfort, of more conventional dress should also be free to wear what they like." The public agreed: 25 years later exhibitionists and "relative anonymists" are still equally welcome in the audience at the Festival Centre.

Right: Adelaide celebrated the magnitude of its achievement

Tight squeeze

In the week before the opening, a PVC downpipe in one of the theatre's toilets became unglued, flooding the foyer. At the time, architect Colin Hassell was considered by his colleagues to have two options open to him: commit hara-kiri, or just die quietly. The builders worked for four days squeegeeing, vacuuming and blow-drying the carpets so they were dry on the night.

Damp dreams

Tony Dawson, of structural engineers Kinnaird, Hill, deRohan & Young, went one better – or worse. The morning of the big day Dawson arrived at the site office in a highly agitated state. He said he dreamt that the building had flooded, and that he had conducted the final inspection with Hassell while standing in five centimetres of water and hoping that the architect wouldn't notice. Many others recall his dream, but Dawson doesn't. "Then again," he says, "I've dreamt about the end of civilisation, and that's what this would have been."

Above: Among the official party –
Margaret and Gough Whitlam, Don
Dunstan and his daughter Bronwyn, Sir
Mark Oliphant and his daughter-in-law
Mrs Michael Oliphant

Gough's encore

During research for the Festival
Centre's 25th anniversary
celebrations, Gough Whitlam
wrote to the Performing Arts
Collection's Jo Peoples. He said
that in many subsequent years
since the opening night, and most
recently at the 1998 Adelaide
Festival, "my wife and I have
shared the joy and pride which
the Adelaide Festival Theatre
has brought to Adelaide, South
Australia and all Australia".

From the start the people of Adelaide had been behind the Festival Theatre,
and the people of Adelaide had got what they deserved.

After the show, more celebration in the foyers. The night was a triumph, said
the Premier in the polo-necked evening shirt. My Government will do more for
the arts than any other, said the latter-day Roman Emperor.

The concert was repeated the following night for the public, to another full
house.

Among the invited guests of 25 years ago, many have only the dimmest
memories of the opening night. They admit they succumbed to the bubbles, and
the euphoria, and mainly both.

They can recall, however, that large groups ended up at the pie cart, still
celebrating the arrival of the Adelaide Festival Centre.

For the right reasons some things had to change in Adelaide, and others
never do.

Lift off

Ruby Litchfield and David Bright were the two Trustees stuck in the lift. They had been in the John Bishop Room and were on their way to the first circle. A front-of-house usher managed to open the doors. "Anthony Steel was very upset," says Dame Ruby. "He was calling out 'You're late. You're late.' But when you're stuck in a lift, you're stuck in a lift. We reached our seats just in time to hear Gough Whitlam open the theatre."

Right: The big stores join the show

Below: Forty thousand South Australians in a single day

Professional party-poopers

For the New Zealand soprano Rosemary Gordon, the opening night was her first *Choral Symphony*. "That made the occasion twice as special for me," she says. "I can recall looking out on the audience, which had a lovely exuberant feeling about it. The hall looked beautiful and our performance went without a hitch." For professional reasons, however, there was no party afterwards for the singers. "We had to repeat the concert the following night," Rosemary says. "We couldn't afford any vocal problems, so we talked as little as possible. But we were thrilled to be part of the wonderful spirit of the night."

CHAPTER 2

"For a comparatively small expenditure . . ."

Forty years ago, Adelaide was not used to debating the arts in public forums.

A former Lord Mayor of Adelaide, Sir Arthur Rymill, changed that when he told the South Australian Upper House: "I do not think the Government is paying sufficient attention to cultural matters . . . I feel that for a comparatively small expenditure we could do something for the State's cultural life".

Eighteen months later the first Adelaide Festival of Arts awakened the city to its cultural life, and alerted the world to its stirrings.

However Sir Arthur wanted more. In October 1960 he informed his political colleagues that the Festival Board of Governors, of which he was a member, had encountered great difficulties finding places in which to present Festival performances.

"The Board respectfully suggests to the Government that a multi-purpose festival hall should be built in Adelaide for the people of South Australia."

The Premier, Sir Thomas Playford, was not noted for his artistic inclinations. He turned down the Board's request for $500,000 to find a place and build a hall. Sir Arthur huffed that the money was small beer compared with $18 million for waterworks and $14 million for government buildings.

You have not heard the last of this, Sir Arthur warned the man known to most South Australians as "Tom."

Tom certainly had not heard the last of it. By October 1963 the festival hall lobby, mainly operating through the Adelaide Establishment and the Town Hall, had worn the Premier down. "All right you can have the thing," Tom said – and his proviso was as straightforward as the man – "as long as it doesn't cost more than a million pounds."

Tom offered $800,000, provided that the Adelaide City Council could find $1million and the public another $200,000. He also made another $200,000 available to buy a site for the hall.

Steele Hall, then a young backbencher and later the Premier who found the

Below: Sir Arthur Rymill "the Board respectfully suggests . . ."

"The least our generation can provide"

Soon after Steele Hall set the site, city tobacconist Laurie Lawrence threw out a challenge. To kick off the public appeal for $100,000 towards a Festival Theatre, Mr Lawrence wrote a letter to *The Advertiser* enclosing $10 with the promise of another $90 when the first $10,000 of the $100,000 was raised. "That way," he wrote, "we'll soon know if anyone else feels as we do – that a Festival Theatre is the least our generation can provide for the future of the city we are proud to belong to." Laurie Lawrence paid full-tote odds, because the appeal met its mark in a week, and then went well past it.

Above: Laurie Lawrence – the first $10

Left: Sir Thomas Playford "All right you can have the thing."

Above: The "covered wagon" proposed for Carclew

Right: Another proposal for the site

Festival Centre site, recalls that the offer seemed at the time "a sort of sop to the arts lobby. I don't think Tom gave a stuff. On the other hand he did it. He made possible what was to come later."

Sop or no sop, the *Festival Hall (City of Adelaide) Act* of 1964 was all the encouragement the arts lobby needed. Within a year the Lord Mayor's Cultural Committee set up by Sir James Irwin had negotiated to buy Carclew, the Bonython family mansion on Montefiore Hill at North Adelaide.

A 2500-seat concert hall suitable also, according to its supporters, for "recitals, mass choral presentations, popular music performances, conventions of all kinds, ice shows, ballet, mime, vaudeville etc." would be built overlooking the city skyline. Theatre facilities would follow later, but "not necessarily in juxtaposition".

But the Festival Hall of the later "covered wagon" design public controversy was not to be. Neither Steele Hall nor Don Dunstan, the Premiers most involved in the creation of the Festival Centre, wanted it at Carclew. Neither did nearby residents, nor the wider performing arts community, which felt it had missed out on the windfall.

The Adelaide City Council, after pushing and prodding the Festival Hall concept through its early years, the Festival Board of Governors and the arts

A CENTRE FOR THE PERFORMING ARTS

JEFFCOTT

lobby learned to live with their disappointment, and with the announcement of the final site all misgivings were removed.

Sir James Irwin proclaimed the selected site feasible and excellent. He also wrote in the Adelaide *News* two days before the opening that the Festival Theatre was the product of cooperation between the Council, all State Governments over the period, and the people of South Australia.

The Festival Theatre was "a great achievement and all those many people who dreamed a dream can now be proud of the reality. It will serve the Adelaide Festival of Arts as it goes from strength to strength for a hundred years – or a thousand years if need be".

Better late than never

It only took 112 years. When Adelaide's historic Institute Building was opened in 1861, the Adelaide *Advertiser* commented, "There ought to be a theatre added to the handsome pile of buildings now erected on North Terrace. A long, lofty, well-ventilated room fitted with galleries and an orchestra, and with a capacity of accommodating 2500 persons, would be a real boon to the public."

CHAPTER 3

Forty-two theatres in 42 days

By early 1969 most parties agreed that Adelaide and South Australia would have a multi-purpose, or lyric, theatre seating 2000 people on the banks of the Torrens in Elder Park.

Apart from that, almost nothing was known. As government briefs go, this one was broad.

Architect Colin Hassell had designed a couple of country halls. At the time, he had "no showbiz" in him.

Acoustic engineer Mike Pryce had played a stringed instrument in the SA Symphony Orchestra in the 1960s, had been a technician with the University Dramatic Society, and had done "few small acoustic things around Adelaide".

The late Russell Arland was Town Clerk of the City of Adelaide, which in 1969 had a managerial stake in any Festival Theatre. The Council decided it had to find out what multi-purpose, or lyric, theatres actually were, and how much they cost to build and operate.

Arland asked Hassell and Pryce to come with him to see the theatres of the world. Given their inexperience, the pair jumped at the idea. Hassell drew up some "rough notional diagrams" and read some technical magazines. Theatre consultant Tom Brown made a list. It consisted of 42 venues in eight countries in 42 days.

In May and June 1969, Arland, Hassell and Pryce paid their own way to see the theatres of the world: Los Angeles, San Francisco, New York, Boston, Montreal, Ottawa, Toronto, Indianapolis, London, Bonn, Frankfurt, Stockholm, Moscow, Tokyo and home to Adelaide via Hong Kong.

"We saw them all," says Hassell today. "At one theatre a day we couldn't really study any of them in depth, but we learnt very quickly. The managers and publicity people would say how marvellous everything was.

"We'd sneak backstage and meet the technicians. Then over a beer we would start to find out what was right and what was wrong."

Far right: Russell Arland and Sir James Irwin

Below: Tom Brown

The Festival Theatre budget was small – by that time about $5 million at an educated guess – and the brief was multi-purpose, so dreams of another Dorothy Chandler Pavilion, New York Metropolitan Opera House, Moscow Palace of Congresses or London Royal Festival Hall were left behind on the ground in Adelaide. However, the grand houses still had to be seen.

In Indianapolis in the United States, the three men saw something not so grand, something they especially liked. Clewes Hall was a multi-purpose theatre with "much to recommend it", they reported to the Adelaide City Council and Premier Steele Hall. "On a limited budget it achieves most requirements for concert, opera and ballet with a minimum of expensive equipment and allows quick transformation from one form to another."

In Montreal the Salle Wilfrid Pelletier was "an excellent theatre providing accommodation similar to Adelaide requirements". The Ottawa National Arts Center, opened in June 1969, had everything planned for the Adelaide Festival Centre one day – opera house and concert hall, small theatre and studio theatre – at a cost of $CAN46.4 million.

"No money has been spared in any departments," the report lamented, and there was more to come. The Frankfurt Opera House employed 120 people full time. "Russell Arland almost fainted," says Mike Pryce. "The Adelaide City Council had proposed a permanent Festival Theatre staff of four."

But by this stage of their journey the three men had reached an agreement: whatever the final shape, the Festival Centre would have to be done properly. "Frankfurt really opened our eyes," says Pryce. "The building, the stage structures, the ramps, the auditorium – everything was made to last 100 years or more.

"While we could not afford a Frankfurt Opera House, the Festival Theatre would be made to last 100 years or more."

Many lessons were learnt in those 42 days.

People are rarely burnt to death in theatre fires. They are trampled to death. The Dorothy Chandler Pavilion doesn't have a centre aisle in the stalls, but each of its three balconies has one. Colin Hassell and Russell Arland sat in the stalls for a performance, Mike Pryce in the first balcony.

After the show the stalls cleared in minutes. Up above, Pryce was still jammed in the aisle. "Continental" seating, with side aisles and generous exits and no centre aisle, would come first to the Festival Theatre, and to Australia, because of that experience. Four years later, during a fire drill at a tuning

Happy landing

Russell Arland, Colin Hassell and Mike Pryce flew non-stop over the Arctic Circle from Moscow to Tokyo on the last leg of their tour. On arrival in Japan civic dignitaries greeted them and young women garlanded them with flowers. "We knew what we were doing was important," says Pryce, "but we didn't realise we were THAT important. Then we were told we had been on the first non-stop flight by the latest model Russian airliner. The Tupolevs didn't have a terrific record for staying in the air then. The Japanese were just glad we had made it and when we found out why, so were we." On such good fortune are great arts centres founded.

Left: John Morphett and Colin Hassell, architects

The continental seating proposed for the Festival Theatre, combined with exhaust fans that would suck smoke away from the audience, removed the need for a cumbersome stage fire curtain, as required by the building act of the time. Overseas, Russell Arland saw the advantages first hand. Back home the City Council and the State Government quietly amended the building act to accommodate the Festival Theatre.

Above: Mike Pryce

concert by the South Australian Symphony Orchestra, the Festival Theatre auditorium was cleared in 60 seconds.

The Theatre stage's floor space is roughly the same as that of the auditorium and no seat is more than 30 metres from the stage. Even in 1969 the joke was already on the Sydney Opera House because of its lack of stage and wing space, and Rudolf Nureyev was later to complain, "One *grand jete* and I'm in Sydney Harbour."

Tom Brown was determined the same disaster wouldn't befall the Festival Theatre, and everywhere Hassell went in 42 days he was advised to make the backstage as large as possible, or the theatre wouldn't work. Thus the largest stage and most successful floor space in Australia at the time would be in the Festival Theatre. It would be several times the size of the Sydney Opera House main stage.

At Clewes Hall Mike Pryce saw his first flyable orchestra shell. At 2000 seats the Festival Theatre would be pushing the acoustic limit for unamplified sound, so it needed a similar shell, able to be flown in and out but still heavy enough to reflect the music of the Israel Philharmonic Orchestra.

The orchestra shell in the Festival Theatre today is an updated version of the one that reflected the sound of the South Australian Symphony Orchestra, 25 years ago.

In the end the Festival Theatre looked nothing like Clewes Hall and cost nothing like the Ottawa National Arts Centre, although eventually it went on to employ more people than the Frankfurt Opera House.

Back home after 42 theatres in 42 days, Colin Hassell was able to report in confidence that plans for an Adelaide Festival Theatre were received "enthusiastically and thought to have excellent possibilities" by theatrical experts in America, Europe and Asia.

"Within the limits provided by the brief and the budget for the Adelaide Festival Theatre it could be said confidently there are no reasons why a world-class theatre cannot be constructed to open in time for the 1972 Festival of Arts . . ."

The architect was one Festival out, but the rest was right on.

CHAPTER 4

Dunstan and Hall, Hall and Dunstan

Labour Premier Don Dunstan, a performing artist in his own right, wanted a South Australian performing arts centre squeezed on the slope between the Torrens Parade Ground and the rear of Government House.

It would have taken a chunk out of the Governor's back yard. The Queen's Representative in South Australia, Sir Edric Bastyan, was not amused, and neither was Dunstan when he asked Federal Army Minister Malcolm Fraser for the Parade Ground.

"We'll sell it to you for $3 million," said Fraser.

"That's outrageous," said Dunstan. "It's a shed. I did my Intermediate exams there."

"That's still our price," said Fraser.

Nothing happened, and as it turned out, just as well.

The Liberals' Steele Hall was a former farm boy. He had no connection with the arts when he won the office of Premier from Dunstan in 1968, although he recalls being outraged by the idea of "the Dunstan squash". Where was the conservation of Colonel Light's Parklands in that proposition?

Hall tended to follow the Liberal party line, which still led to Montefiore Hill at North Adelaide and Carclew. But he had grown uneasy about the site. Was it too far from the centre of the city? It was directly under the Adelaide Airport flight path. There had been criticism of its exclusivity as a concert music venue at the expense of the other performing arts. Dunstan had whipped up the controversy while in Opposition.

Hall was in London promoting South Australian industry when an engagement fell through, and an official suggested he might take a look at London's Royal Festival Hall, down by the River Thames. "Might as well," the Premier said to the SA House driver.

Off they went. "I was shown over the complex of three halls," Hall says. "While I had little expertise to gauge their effectiveness, I was nevertheless

Steele Hall "I'm proud to have done my bit."

Don't come the raw prawn, Mr Premier . . .

Steele Hall had asked Prime Minister John Gorton for tax concessions for the public appeal for the future Festival Theatre. Hall was staggered when he was turned down. State Government members continued to lobby the Prime Minister's Office. The Premier's dinner at the Highway Inn on Anzac Highway was interrupted by a phone call. It was the Prime Minister, on a prawn boat in the Gulf of Carpentaria. "I don't know how Gorton found me at the Highway Inn," Hall says, "or what he was doing on a prawn boat, but he gave me a real serve. Then when he finished he said I could have the tax concessions or $100,000. He wanted to know right now. In haste I took the $100,000. It seems such a piddling amount now. I still wonder if I should have taken the tax concessions. It could have been a toss up."

Right: Adelaide 1906. On the left, Dunstan's site; on the right Hall's.

impressed with their location next to the Thames. The vista of water was an additional dimension to stone and mortar and was a thought-starter about our running controversy back home.

"I began thinking about getting the Festival Theatre near the Torrens somewhere."

Hall had to work fast on his return home. In his absence, his Cabinet and the Adelaide City Council had agreed to build a Festival Hall at Carclew. The announcement was meant to end the years of uncertainty.

Top: City and site, 1934

Above: The Cheer Up Hut, 1918

"My Cabinet colleagues were proud that they had negotiated and fixed the Carclew site and set the financial parameters," Hall says. "I myself was shocked at what governments can get up to while the boss is away."

The next Sunday Hall took a stroll around the city. On King William Road at the southern end of Elder Park, the old City Baths were still in use but the Adelaide Aquatic Centre in the North Parklands would soon supersede them.

The rest was a mishmash – a fibro migrant hostel, the World War I and II Cheer Up Hut, the Elder Park kiosk, *The Advertiser* Sound Shell and an occasional sanctuary for the homeless. But the land sloped gently down to the Torrens.

This was the spot, Hall decided, right in the middle of Adelaide. "Why had it taken so long for any of us to work this out?

"A certain amount of discreet individual lobbying of my colleagues, broached firmly and diplomatically, was needed to re-open the question they were so pleased to have settled. I was agreeably surprised when the reversal was accomplished without apparent ill feeling.

"It was a pretty swift act. The Carclew site couldn't be allowed to go on."

From that moment on, it was as though everyone was relieved. "The cooperation of the City Council was outstanding," Hall says. "Everyone loved the site. Even Dunstan dropped his opposition to it after about 10 days. There didn't seem to be a single fly in the ointment.

"The Festival Theatre could never go up at Carclew. It had to be central, and since those days the central effect of Adelaide has become more accentuated." Hall says.

"The architects produced a balsa model for Cabinet. It suited the site perfectly. I was sorry the main entrance couldn't be by the water's edge, but obviously you couldn't build the stage up the hill. *The Advertiser* agreed to demolish the Sound Shell, and the walkway by the river was my suggestion.

"The late sixties was a time when natural protagonists would gather around and help with projects. I doubt whether the Festival Theatre could be built today."

Dunstan had the 1968 report by New York theatre consultant Thomas DeGaetani still fresh in his mind when he became Premier again in 1970. DeGaetani had recommended a 2000-seat lyric theatre/concert hall with variable acoustics, a 700-seat drama theatre, an experimental space, exhibition and gallery areas, and adequate dressing rooms and workshops.

A performing arts complex along DeGaetani's lines, on Steele Hall's site, where work had already begun, would accommodate both the Festival and the Premier's envisaged State-funded theatre, opera and dance companies. In August 1971 Dunstan announced the full go-ahead.

In answer to Hall's question about the time taken to find the site, when DeGaetani surveyed Adelaide's semi-arid arts landscape in early 1968, an underground railway was planned for King William Street; the City Baths were still an Adelaide landmark, much of the site was owned by the South Australian Railways; and one of the city's main sewers ran directly underneath. For DeGaetani, Elder Park was not an option.

Top: City Baths

Above: *The Advertiser* Sound Shell

The underground railway had been dumped by 1970 and the Aquatic Centre would soon replace the City Baths. There were ways around sewers, and Dunstan would find a way around the SA Railways.

Dunstan liked the Festival Theatre idea but decided the City Council had neither the money to finish a full Festival Centre project, nor the expertise to control it. He passed legislation to create the Adelaide Festival Centre Trust, giving the City Council two seats on it.

FESTIVAL HALL

ARTS COMPLEX

The original Adelaide Festival Centre Trust comprised chairman John Baily, Dame Ruby Litchfield, composer Richard Meale and Judge John Roder, with James Bowen and David Bright from the City Council.

"I wanted people who were acquainted with the arts and had some managerial experience, yet were not major players amongst potential users of the Centre," Dunstan says.

"The Trust was provided with a semi-government loan, then instructed to proceed with planning of the remainder of the Centre as DeGaetani conceived it, and to create a plaza area between the Centre and the back of Parliament House."

To plan the Centre's second building – the drama theatre, experimental space and gallery – Dunstan had to take over more railways land than Hall had previously negotiated for the Festival Theatre. The Railways Institute would have to go.

The Premier fronted the SA Railways Commissioner, Ron Fitch, with the proposition.

"The Commissioner told me it was his duty to protect Railways assets," Dunstan says. "I looked at him and shouted, 'GO AWAY AND DO IT!'

"There was much protest from Steele Hall by the way. He said the rest of the Centre was a waste of money."

Dunstan called in the theatre consultant Tom Brown, who had played Sebastian to Dunstan's Malvolio in Adelaide theatrical identity Colin Ballantyne's first post-War production of *Twelfth Night*. Brown had worked for many years in London, where he came under the influence of the director Tyrone Guthrie.

The Festival Centre was under way. Don Dunstan, the performing artist in his own right, was in his element.

At the Festival Theatre opening, Dunstan acknowledged Hall's part in setting the site and initiating work on the theatre building.

Steele Hall, the former farm boy, wasn't there. "Dunstan was the man of the arts," Hall says today. "I've never been that close to the arts, but I'm proud to have done my bit for them in South Australia."

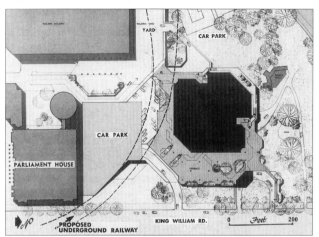

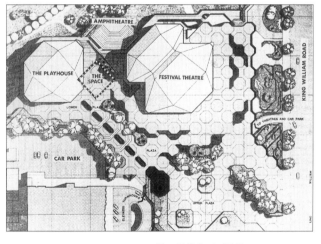

Top: Hall's Festival Hall

Above: Dunstan's Festival Centre

Left: Dunstan gives the full go-ahead

CHAPTER 5

A general manager, via Algiers

Len Amadio had been Premier Don Dunstan's arts right-hand man for only a few months in 1971 when a friend offered him a free seat on an Alitalia inaugural flight from Milan to Algiers.

Milan to Algiers? Amadio didn't want to go to Algiers. He wanted to go to London to hear some music and find a general manager for the Adelaide Festival Centre now taking shape by the Torrens. Around 100 applicants for the job from Australia, the United Kingdom and the United States had impressed neither him nor Dunstan.

But the free trip was a generous and tempting offer all the same.

Amadio was given leave without pay. He flew to Milan, caught the inaugural flight to Algiers where he stayed in the airport's transit lounge, and took the first plane back to Milan. He then flew on to London at his own expense. "The worst flight of my life," Amadio recalls, "charging over the Alps in a snowstorm. I couldn't sleep. I was a wreck when I arrived, but the pilot would've been too."

He called on Sir Ian Hunter, an international adviser to Adelaide Festivals of Arts since the first in 1960. Was there anyone available who was equal to the task of setting up and running a multi-purpose performing arts complex on the other side of the world?

"I was told there was only one person I really must see: Anthony Steel, head of programming at South Bank Concert Hall. 'He's in his thirties and brilliant, brilliant.'" Amadio rang the conductor Daniel Barenboim, who was giving a concert with the London Philharmonic Orchestra at South Bank that night.

"Danny, I'd love to come to the concert," Amadio said, "and also to meet Anthony Steel." Barenboim replied that Steel normally buzzed around backstage in the interval. "Try then."

The pair met. "Len Amadio from Adelaide, Mr Steel. How are you going? Love to have a chat with you about a job. I'm only here for three days. I'm going up

The right stuffed

Before his appointment was decided, Anthony Steel came to Adelaide from London to meet the Festival Centre Trust. The Trustees took him to dinner at the Magic Flute, then back to Jim Bowen's house at North Adelaide for coffee. Steel had flown in that day. "I'm awfully tired," he told his hosts, and went to sleep on the floor between two lounge chairs. That didn't worry the Trustees. "We decided we had a man who knew his own mind," says David Bright, "and we were right".

Left: Anthony Steel – "the answer to my prayers"

25

Above: Len Amadio

to the Aldeburgh Festival on Sunday, and flying out of London on Monday."

Steel was going to the Aldeburgh Festival too. "Let's have lunch there."

The two talked for an hour. "Anthony expressed great interest," says Amadio, "and we got along very well. He said he wasn't available until the following year. I told him the position would be re-advertised and he would get a copy of the ad. The position of artistic director of the Festival might also be involved. I would have to clear all this with the Premier."

Steel recalls a sense of "this might be the right thing to do at the time". Amadio went on to the three o'clock concert of Sir Benjamin Britten conducting the English Chamber Orchestra in the Maltings confident he had found what the Festival Centre was looking for.

Back in Adelaide, Amadio began to worry when he hadn't heard from Steel after a month. Then Jean Battersby, executive officer of the Australia Council, told him if he wanted Anthony Steel for Adelaide, he'd better get him now.

"He was on the short-list for the Sydney Opera House job," Amadio recalls. "Some bastard in London had recommended him."

Amadio sent a telegram asking Steel to meet Dunstan at South Australia House in The Strand. Steel replied: "You've twisted my arm. I shall walk across Waterloo Bridge." He asked for both jobs – Festival Centre general manager and Festival artistic director. Dunstan knew the Festival Board wanted to advertise for a separate director.

In 1972 the Festival required a $100,000 bailout from the State Government. It was the lever Dunstan needed. Pressure was applied to the Festival Board. Steel missed out on the Opera House job. Instead he guided the Adelaide Festival Centre through its first five formative years and revived the Adelaide Festival.

"I came to Adelaide with some degree of trepidation," Steel says today, "and it turned out to be the answer to my prayers."

Len Amadio never went back to the transit lounge at Algiers Airport. He never needed to, once he had delivered Anthony Steel to Adelaide.

CHAPTER 6

It'll be all right on the roof

Architect John Morphett asked his senior partner Colin Hassell to come and see his pencil sketch.

"I think this is it, Colin," Morphett said. "This is how the Festival Theatre is going to look."

That night Morphett went home and made a small cardboard model. It was of two octahedrons – a tall skinny one for the stage tower and a broad fat one for the auditorium and foyer. They intersected on the theatre's proscenium.

Next morning everyone in the office agreed with Morphett. The Adelaide City Council and the State Government followed soon after. Compared with the growing pains of the Sydney Opera House, Adelaide would have its Festival Theatre just like that.

Below: The broad fat octahedron

Right: Dennis Smith, left, with Sir Asher Joel, of the Sydney Opera House

Below: Site architect Bruce Harry – designed from the inside out

The Theatre was designed from the inside out. The octahedrons on the 45-degree angle to the main pattern of Adelaide streets were a response to the already planned stage, auditorium and continental seating, and to the site itself. "We wanted the theatre to relate to the rest of the city while following the slope of the land," Morphett says.

That was in 1969. Four years would pass before opening night. The challenge to get there on time was not unique to theatre design and construction, but it was protean: the Festival Theatre had to be many things to many audiences and many performers – a concert hall, an opera house, a music theatre, a convention centre, a cinema. It meant many hands would be involved. Though the hands were skilled, they had never worked on anything like this before.

The 100-year-old sewer serving Adelaide's CBD was realigned. Instead of running under J Row, the sewer now skirts Lyrics Restaurant. "It was a big job," says Fred Flood of SA Water. "The Engineering and Water Supply Department made a more definitive space for the Festival Theatre."

The Theatre alone has eight kilometres of air-conditioning ducts, 240 kilometres of electrical wiring, 2500 square metres of glass and 10,000 metres of carpet. It weighs 30,000 tonnes and stands on an ancient mud bank of the Torrens. The builder, A.V. Jennings, drove 600 concrete piles through the mud to gravel and siltstone beds.

In early 1972 Don Dunstan appointed Dennis Smith, an Adelaide builder and theatre technician, as the Theatre's technical manager. Smith was the Adelaide Festival Centre Trust's first employee. He worked out of Trust chairman John Baily's office at the Art Gallery of South Australia.

"Those were 100-hour weeks in a pressure cooker," says Smith, now a film art director and designer in Sydney. "The enthusiasm was amazing. Yet even so it was equally amazing the place opened on time.

"We all had pieces of knowledge which we had to bring together. That somehow we did was the great joy of those early days. Most of those days it was madness."

Smith monitored all staging and theatre-building operations and services, liaising with the architect and the builder. Early on the City Council considered cost-cutting. The cheapest option was a concrete stage floor.

Dancers would never have danced again after dancing at the Festival Theatre. Oak was considered next. Local bone surgeons would have had to miss their after-show suppers to treat dancers who tried to dance on solid oak. Smith changed the floor to pine with a flexible Masonite covering.

Cold comfort

While the story of the making of the Festival Centre is regarded as one of cooperation and understanding all round, there were some close calls. Any government, even a 1970s Dunstan Government, is wary of spending in areas alien to it. At one time State Cabinet considered installing only cold water taps in the Festival Theatre foyer bars and toilets.

What had to go to get it

The quaintest casualty of the Adelaide Festival Centre was the "warming shed". The South Australian Railways kept a boiler and racks of brass hot-water bottles in a tin hut by the Torrens. The brass bottles warmed the feet of first-class passengers on the Overland train to Melbourne. Architects and construction workers alike were sad to see the "warming shed" go.

Opposite top: The Jonas Hungarian Gypsy Orchestra tests the appreciation of the hard hats – the theatre's first musical performance
Opposite below: Many hands involved

Where the Festival Centre might have been

Besides Carclew and the area behind Government House, several sites were considered for an Adelaide Festival Hall or Theatre. One was Government House itself, with the Governor moving to Carclew. Others included Botanic Park, the East End Market, Hindmarsh Square, the Adelaide Railway Station yards, the tram barn in Victoria Square, and the southern half of Victoria Square.

The most radical proposal was to close off King William Road at South Terrace, and build the theatre in the South Parklands. The siting of Bonython Hall at the termination of Pulteney Street inspired the idea. The rear of Government House site was to have tunnels with moving walkways under the Vice-Regal Residence connecting it to the parking stations of North Terrace.

Right: Adelaide's skyline changes for art's sake

The first film projectors barely raised a flicker on the Theatre's cinema screen. The stage didn't have work lights. The scenery flying lines were incompatible with any other theatre in Australia. Four months were spent locating a noise in a cooling tower. There was nowhere to put the rubbish.

"To say we were all on a steep learning curve is an understatement," Smith says.

Everywhere there was compromise, not usually the best approach, but this was an exception. Acoustics engineer Mike Pryce had to tread the fine line between sound and comfort. "The theatre's finish had to be luxurious," he says, "so we had to have all the carpet.

"Today I would've jumped up and down about the amount of sound absorption for symphony concerts, yet that was the compromise of a multi-purpose theatre. We knew from the start there would be that compromise."

So it was a mixture of madness and compromise from the start – compromise and creative madness and a great big risk that paid off. In the end though, the theatre world is about creative madness.

When Smith saw the American performance artist Charlotte Moorman naked on the roof of John Morphett's intersecting octahedrons playing a blue-dyed ice cello hanging from a fishing line, he knew the madness in the creation of the Adelaide Festival Centre made sense.

As she played, the cello melted on to a metal plate, where a contact microphone picked up the sound of water dripping. It was mad enough for Dennis Smith to realise it had all been worthwhile.

Right: Charlotte Moorman and the intersecting octahedrons

CHAPTER 7

Winnie the Pooh
and a sea of smiling faces

"Wherever I am there's always Pooh, There's always Pooh and Me." On 17 December 1973, 15-year-old Andrew Roffe as Christopher Robin sang the first words in the first production by the Adelaide Festival Centre Trust.

A.A. Milne's *Winnie the Pooh* was presented at the Festival Theatre by the Trust and SAS Channel 10 in association with Harry M. Miller. It was described in the program by general manager Anthony Steel as the Trust's "most ambitious venture yet. We have been constantly aware since the Festival Theatre opened in June, of the need to bring as wide a variety of theatre fare as possible to the people of Adelaide, and one of our greatest concerns has been for younger audiences."

Above: Yana Taylor, Sue Wylie, Noni Hazlehurst, Mandy Hughs-Jones, Rainer Jozeps, Peter Braendler and John Greene in *Winnie the Pooh*

Actor and television presenter Noni Hazlehurst, then a starry-eyed young Flinders University drama student, was a fieldmouse, in a head-to-toe furry suit and big clumpy shoes. Before Andrew Roffe sang, the cast had to pretend to be asleep in the woods. At the first performance Noni opened her eyes and saw a "sea of smiling faces.

"We could see the children. That meant they could see us. It was a great relief in a place as large as the Festival Theatre. I remember how extraordinarily clean the theatre was, and the fresh excitement about it. *Winnie the Pooh* went on to be a delightful production and I was thrilled to be in it, in my first professional role.

Left and above: "We were always laughing."

"Looking back now, I realise that our audiences reflected the public acceptance of the Festival Theatre. It quickly gained success and authenticity within the city. It became much-loved because it was much-needed, too."

The show ran for four weeks and starred Wally Carr as Pooh Bear, Elaine Cusick as Piglet, Ian Boyce as Owl, and Roffe, who later joined Australian Opera and who died in 1993. Adelaide theatrical agent Ann Peters was a chorus rabbit. "We were always laughing," she says. "The temperaments of the actors and the enthusiasm of the audience made *Winnie the Pooh* a very happy show."

Michael Scheid was Tigger. He was conscious that he was a part of making history at the Festival Theatre. "I was very aware that this was our first very own show at our very own theatre. As the bouncing tiger I broke my toe and had to go to the Royal Adelaide Hospital. But I still did every show. I wasn't going to miss any of it."

For the following Christmas holiday season the Trust presented Gilbert and Sullivan's *The Gondoliers* and *The Mikado*, showcasing Dennis Olsen, at the Festival Theatre and *Holiday on Ice* at the Playhouse. The Trust's first production, its "most ambitious venture yet" would lead to more ambitious ventures.

At the end of 1977 came *Ned Kelly*. But for Michael Scheid *Winnie the Pooh* was the beginning of the magic. "We played to full houses every morning and afternoon. Our own show in Adelaide at the Festival Theatre was such fun we hoped it would never end."

Mornings with the Mels

Not long after *Winnie the Pooh*, Wally Carr and Marie Fidock began a popular Festival Centre tradition of morning senior citizens concerts that continues today. The concerts became known as "Morning Melodies" in 1986, and the 12,000 seats in each of two seasons a year are a sell-out. They are marketed mainly to retired people by brochures and word-of-mouth only. The "Morning Mels" are regarded as one of the direct mail success stories of Australian entertainment marketing.

CHAPTER 8

Her Majesty gives the Royal Seal

The Queen and Prince Phillip arrived at the brand new $5.8 million Festival Centre Southern Plaza from across the road at Government House at 4.05 p.m.

A young man waving the Eureka flag and shouting "Independence for Australia" appeared on the official dais. He hit the red gravel near the Hajek environmental sculpture under a crush of police.

"He will be a very sore boy," said a detective.

The Queen stared straight ahead. The wind whipped up the red dust.

A group protesting against the Hajek sculpture handed out leaflets and carried banners bearing the words "Australian art? Who decides?"

At 4.16 p.m. Premier Don Dunstan's welcoming speech was drowned out by eight planes from the Royal Aero Club of SA. Royal Australian Air Force signalmen who were supposed to give the planes the all-clear for the fly-past never appeared on the roof of Parliament House.

In his speech the Premier commented that since the Queen's accession to the throne there had been great and complex changes in the organisation of communities throughout the world. But one characteristic of British and Australian life had not altered – and that was the public respect and affection commanded by Her Majesty.

Dunstan remarked that the Hajek sculpture would enhance and complement the architecturally rich precincts of the Festival Centre, Parliament House, the old Legislative Council chamber and the Railways Building.

Any protest against the Hajek was like protesting about Michelangelo painting the Sistine Chapel. The protestors moaned loudly.

The Queen stared straight ahead. She then thanked South Australians for their loyalty and friendship. The Festival Centre was a spectacular addition to Adelaide's cultural life, she said, and would increase still further the city's stature and reputation as a centre of the performing arts.

Her Majesty was also very pleased that the people of South Australia had chosen to commemorate her visit by buying a pipe organ. "May the 'pealing organ' blow for many years to come to the delight of all who hear it."

A commemorative plaque was unveiled. On Tuesday 22 March 1977, after seven years of building and $25.5 million, the Adelaide Festival Centre was finally and officially completed.

The Queen pressed a button to start a flow of water from the Olga Lodge fountain to a series of fountains leading to the Playhouse. Those of the 10,000 spectators standing in the fountain unaware that it was a fountain, were drenched.

The fountain had to be turned off.

By 4.42 p.m. the Royal couple was safely inside in the Festival Centre.

"At least it didn't rain," said Festival Centre marketing head Tony Frewin.

CHAPTER 9

"A huge place in my life"

Anthony Steel had a deep love and knowledge of western classical music. He spoke Russian. He could sing, dance, play the clarinet and operate puppets.

But his knowledge of theatre was confined to what he had picked up sitting in the audience at the Royal Court near his Chelsea home. Anthony Steel had never run a theatre – let alone four – when he arrived in Adelaide to take over the Adelaide Festival Centre.

"I was absolutely terrified," Steel says. "The Trust had one employee, Dennis Smith, and I knew what the buildings were going to look like. Otherwise it was entirely up to me."

Steel was a quick learner. His first year at an arts centre that had not yet

Right: Anthony Steel with *The Australian's* Geraldine Pascal

opened was a crash course in theatre and the arts. Steel picked brains. He absorbed the ideas fed him by other people. He admits he relied on the theatre consultant Tom Brown "enormously".

He networked. He begged and demanded. When it was realised that the Festival Theatre would not have enough scenery flylines for the touring national companies, Steel went to Premier Don Dunstan. The Festival Theatre would not be first and best if the Australian Opera and Australian Ballet could not perform there.

"You will have the cheque for the flytower by the end of next week," Dunstan promised.

Steel was volatile. His Englishness and intellect was seen as arrogance in some quarters. In others, his presence and authority won concessions for the Trust, and changes for the Centre. He was popular with his staff because he made things happen.

Throughout the lead-up to the opening of the Festival Theatre, Steel was confident he had the support of everyone involved. "I never felt alone," he says. "We were all so excited about creating something new for Adelaide."

At the same time Steel became a successful Adelaide Festival director almost overnight. He used his linguistic skills to open doors to the arts in Eastern Europe and the Soviet Union. He represented the arts of today and the future, not yesterday.

In four and a half years, for all his volatility and his quirks, Steel delivered four operational theatres to Adelaide and brought style and panache to the Festival Centre. He was its permanent public performance, liable to be playing any day.

In 1977, Steel decided he had done all he could do. "What I saw and heard from the public of South Australia, and my response to it, convinced me it was getting a bit unhealthy. It was time I left."

Others within the Centre, led by Kevin Earle and Tony Frewin, agreed that Steel should leave. They had been of this opinion for some time.

Steel stayed to present the 1978 Festival, then went on to other festivals and other arts positions in Australia and other countries. But, he says, "The most important time of my life was spent in Adelaide between 1972 and 1978. Sixty per cent of that time was spent inside the Festival Centre. It has a huge place in my life. It affected everything I did after that, and it affects my thoughts still."

In 1998, the year of the 25th anniversary of the Adelaide Festival Theatre, Anthony Steel chose to live in Adelaide again.

Dressing down

Anthony Steel's celebrated kaftan was not a kaftan at all. It was a man's summer dressing gown bought for $30 at David Jones. Steel wore it with sandals as a send-up of Biblical dress to the Adelaide premiere of *Jesus Christ Superstar* at the Festival Theatre in 1975. He only appeared in public in it half a dozen times, but in 1970s Adelaide that was enough to cause a fuss. The "kaftan" ended in a bin in 1997.

Twin virtues

Teena Munn, former secretary to the Adelaide Festival: "Anthony was one of my mentors. He taught me tolerance and patience. You needed tolerance and patience with Anthony Steel, and he wouldn't deny it."

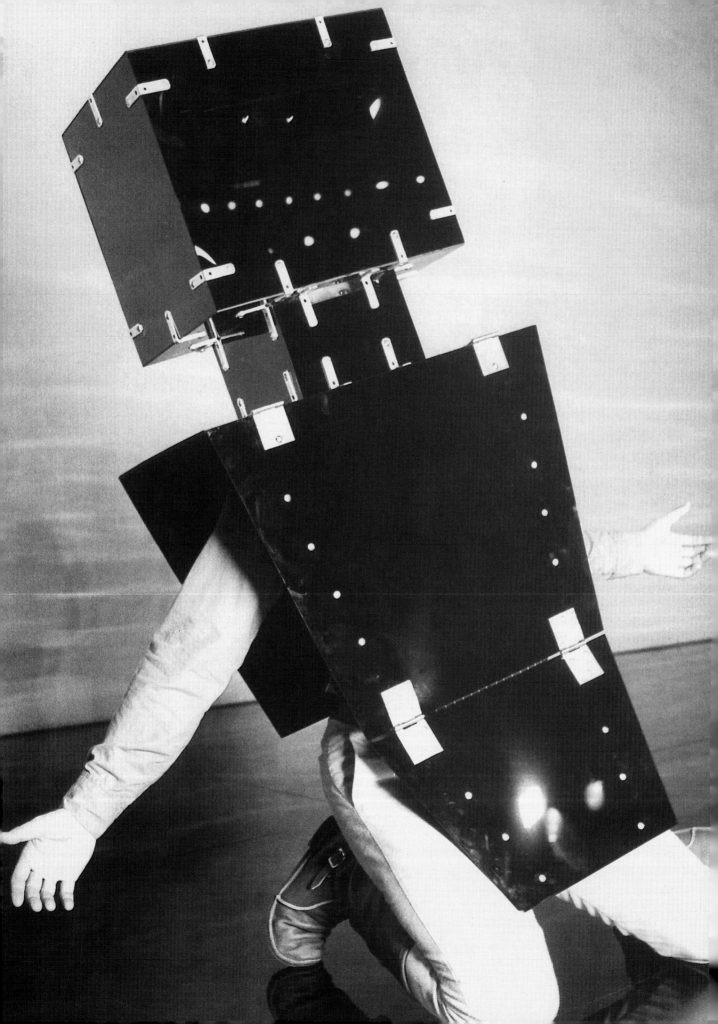

CHAPTER 10

Too game for Ned Kelly?

He was so famous that Australians knew him as Ned.

Ned Kelly.

He was so famous that Australians knew him as Reg.

Reg Livermore.

Ned and Reg, Australia's greatest folk legend and Australia's finest popular theatre artist would combine to produce what Livermore promised would be "the biggest thing that has happened in Australian theatre".

Friday 30 December 1977 was to be the night of nights, the Festival Theatre the place for a milestone in the young life of the Adelaide Festival Centre Trust. The world premiere of *Ned Kelly*, mounted at a price of $250,000, would launch the Trust as a major theatrical entrepreneur on a national scale.

The theatrical experience of *Ned Kelly* did much more than that. Adelaide would never be a peaceful, law-abiding arts town again. The Kelly Gang itself couldn't have done it better at Glenrowan. Shots were exchanged. For the first time, theatre criticism and arts politics hit the front pages.

For the last time for him, Livermore decided soon after. "This might be Adelaide, but it's my Dallas." He swore he wasn't coming back.

It all started quietly. In the program for *Ned Kelly – The Electric Music Show*, general manager Kevin Earle wrote "to ensure maximum use of our theatres, the Trust, through its entrepreneurial wing, pursues an energetic programme of producing and presenting a wide range of theatre entertainment.

"The enormous cost, however, of mounting major productions has made it clear that at some stage the Trust would have to extend itself beyond Adelaide and present its shows to a wider audience. We wanted to be sure that when that time came the show would be a winner."

The Trust met half the cost of *Ned Kelly*. Thirty-eight other major and minor investors provided the rest. Reg Livermore would provide the genius, as writer, designer and director. His one-man shows, *Betty Blokk Buster Follies* and

THE ADVERTISER

Above: Reg Livermore – "A smack in the face."

Left: "The most spectacular Australian musical for 20 years."

Above: Shirley Stott Despoja – "You would have thought I'd said there was no God."

Ned Spaghetti

Many people believed *Ned Kelly* was ahead of its time, except for one thing. In the all-singing, all-dancing electric musical, the performers used eight hand-held microphones, each attached to 20-metre cables. A casual stagehand was employed to untangle the "spaghetti" a dozen times a night. "It was an absolute nightmare – like dancing on an electric maypole," Trust production manager Denise Lovick remembers. *Ned Kelly* might not have been a box-office success, but it was a miracle its cast survived it intact, or even alive. The safer radio body microphones came to the Festival Theatre for the first time two years later with *Evita*.

Wonder Woman, had confirmed his huge appeal with Australian audiences in the mid-1970s.

A largely unknown cast would provide the talent, youth and energy. Two years earlier Nick Turbin was a "singing plumber" around Sydney. Now he would play Ned Kelly in what the Trust boasted would be "the most spectacular Australian musical to be seen for 20 years".

The Trust was on a winner, it was sure.

Shirley Stott Despoja, the arts editor of the Adelaide *Advertiser*, cast doubts on this claim. The Wednesday after the world premiere Stott Despoja wrote that *Ned Kelly* was a "fiasco", "an artistic disaster", "a hideous monument to bad taste and theatrical excess".

The Trust had given Livermore "a ridiculous amount of money to spend on a show that says money, money, money and very little else". Stott Despoja questioned the use of public funds to stage *Ned Kelly* and pay for the first night party in a train shed at Mile End. ". . . a $¼ million mistake followed by a $4000 celebration is something even a government would be called to account over, let alone the Festival Centre which was the major entrepreneur . . ."

And, "When I think of what the SA Theatre Company, the State Opera or the Australian Dance Theatre could have done with the amount of money wasted on lighting the show alone, I could weep."

Earle returned fire in *The Advertiser* next day. He defended the Trust's role as an entrepreneur: "*Ned Kelly* was produced to fill our major need of the year – a period of six to eight weeks in the Festival Theatre when other hirers and entrepreneurs are not interested in taking a risk."

As for the choice of *Ned Kelly*, Earle wrote, "Of course we could keep on doing Gilbert and Sullivan ad infinitum, or pull out a few old 'safe' and hoary chestnuts and completely abdicate any responsibility we might feel to Australian creativity or the Australian experience."

For Livermore, the creator, *Ned Kelly* was the first serious victim of Adelaide arts politics involving the use of taxpayers' money. "It was a smack in the face for me," he says. "I still think of Ned as a tremendous attempt, and it was brave of the Trust to support us.

"I suppose the show was flawed. It had directorial mistakes. I dare say if it had been given a fair assessment I might have tried to fix it. But it wasn't. It was a very sobering experience, the way it was torn apart by the arts editor of the time."

Twenty years on, Stott Despoja says she "will not retract a word of it. I made a lot of enemies. You'd have thought I had said there was no God. The

Trust was spending public money like water. The other critics disagreed violently with me.

"Adelaide had had Festival censorship debates before, but here was critical opinion becoming front page. It was justified with *Ned Kelly*. It was the beginning of Adelaide as a place for serious public consideration of the arts."

Ned Kelly saw out its Adelaide season with a loss then limped to Sydney, where Livermore heard people say, "Don't bother to go to it – it's a flop."

Livermore overcame his aversion to his "Dallas". He returned to the Festival Theatre five years later for *Barnum*, and later *Sacred Cow II*. He might even return to *Ned Kelly*. "The show had as many fans as detractors," he says, "but it couldn't take the hostility. There were a lot of fabulous things in it. I could probably reorganise it. Someone asked me about *Ned* just the other day."

Below: Production manager John Robertson with part of the set – "a $1/4 million mistake" or a "tremendous attempt"?

High flying, and adored

The Adelaide Festival Centre Trust ordered its general manager Kevin Earle to acquire the Australian rights to *Evita*. This suited Earle – he had told the Trust to order him to get *Evita* in the first place.

Earle wanted "the biggest musical ever mounted" more than anything else he had wanted for the Festival Centre. In early 1978 *Ned Kelly* had lost $300,000, yet it had been a creative beginning. Then had come the turnaround. Adelaide seasons had saved the Australian tours of the play *Dracula* and the musical *Annie* and restored the Trust's confidence.

With his programming manager Tony Frewin, Earle had worked out their audience. "We know our city and we know how to promote in our city," he said, and Adelaide would adore *Evita*. The rest of Australia would follow. He would fly anywhere to secure it.

The Andrew Lloyd Webber–Tim Rice musical had dominated London's West End for two years. Its signature song, "Don't Cry For Me Argentina", was a pop anthem of the late 1970s. *Evita* had not yet opened on Broadway when Earle met Robert Stigwood, the owner of the rights.

Stigwood was South Australian-born, and his mother Gwen Burrows lived in Adelaide. The man who had made his millions with *Hair* and *Jesus Christ Superstar* in London and New York, and with *Saturday Night Fever* and *Grease* in Hollywood, may have been susceptible to sentiment, but the Trust had its competitors.

Everybody else wanted *Evita* – Michael Edgley International, the Elizabethan Theatre Trust and Kenn Brodziak. The Trust's then operations manager John Robertson recalls the meticulous planning that went into negotiating the rights. "Kevin, Tony and I put together the Trust's credentials to the letter," he says. "We left nothing out.

"One day we decided it was time for Kevin to go to London, and he went. There was no other way. It had to be face-to-face with Stigwood."

Earle was a hard-nosed businessman who absolutely loved show business,

Prince of pratfalls

Hal Prince was already an American musical theatre legend when he came to Adelaide in 1980 to direct *Evita*. He had directed or produced among many others *Fiddler on the Roof* and *A Little Night Music*. During an *Evita* preview the set's cinema screen jammed. Prince leapt from his seat into the wings. He hurtled across the stage, tripped on a raised section and slid the rest of the way flat on his face. Prince stopped the show. "Who's that clown?" asked a member of the audience. "Couldn't direct traffic," said someone who knew. Hal Prince had become an Adelaide musical theatre legend too.

Right: John O'May as Che Guevara

Opposite page: Robert Stigwood, Hal Prince and Andrew Lloyd Webber – the best *Evita* yet

Basil and Ru

The Advertiser's long-time arts columnist Basil Arty, playful chronicler of goings-on at the Festival Centre for 13 years, was at the *Evita* party. Needing a break from the high jinks he slipped below to the Old Lion's underground bar. In a far corner he espied a solitary figure. "Having a rest from the party?" the artist formerly known as Basil inquired. "Yes, a lot of noise up there," replied Rupert Murdoch. "Great show though, *Evita*." "Yes, great show." And that was that – the only time the two legends of Australian journalism ever met.

says Robertson. So too was Stigwood. *Evita*, at the end of the 1970s, was the ultimate in show business. Stigwood and Earle were on common ground.

Even with the added attraction of Adelaide being Stigwood's home town, the winning of *Evita* was "an absolute coup for Kevin Earle and the Trust", says Robertson. "We had to prove we could actually get it on, because the original creative team was to come to Adelaide.

"The Trust's production of *Evita* had to be as good as London's or New York's, or better. The excitement it generated carried everyone along."

The excitement paid off at the box office. On the eve of the Australian premiere of *Evita* at the Festival Theatre, more than $500,000 in bookings had been sold – a cash advance record for an Australian theatre to that time, and more than for the world premiere in London two years before.

The night of Wednesday 30 April 1980, was a landmark in Australian theatre history. All eyes were on Adelaide. It was the city's biggest night out at a single show. Lloyd Webber and Rice were in the first-night audience along with Stigwood and Rupert Murdoch.

Adelaide had never before seen the likes of the opening-night party afterwards at the Old Lion Hotel. It had not ended at dawn.

Kevin Earle was "euphoric", says Robertson. "We all were. We were just beginning to comprehend the magnitude of what we had done."

Like the song in the show, *Evita* was high-flying, and adored. Extra performances were arranged for the Adelaide season. When it finished playing Perth *Evita* had recovered its major production and transportation costs. By the time it reached Melbourne it was almost in the black.

The organisation that set out to manage a performing arts centre had become a major producer and entrepreneur in its own right. From now on the Adelaide Festival Centre Trust was in showbiz, big time.

Evita cost the Trust and its partners $850,000. The Trust made a million dollars, which it used to stage more musicals. "*Evita* started everything up to this day," says John Robertson of what Andrew Lloyd Webber declared was the best production of *Evita* he had seen.

Better than London, better than New York, and worth the plane trip.

THE ADVERTISER

At the final preview the costume dressing gown worn by Peter Carroll as Juan Peron became stuck in the scenery during the "I'd Be Surprisingly Good For You" duet with Jennifer Murphy as Eva Duarte. Nothing Carroll could do would budge it. The actors were wearing radio mikes for the first time in an Australian production. Carroll sang:

"I can (rip) understand you perfectly (riipp),

"And I like what I hear (riiippp), what I see (riiipppp), and knowing me,

"I would be good (riiiippppp) for you too (riiiiiiiiippppppppp)."

Peron broke free, his gown in shreds. The next night, the grand gala Australian charity premiere performance, Carroll wore the same dressing gown, stitched and patched. With economies like that, no wonder the biggest musical ever mounted in Australia to that time made a million dollars.

It's my party

Robert Stigwood paid for the opening night party at the Old Lion. And that meant everything. Not until around 3.30 a.m. did a Stigwood assistant step in to prevent guests booking up their cigarettes to the Robert Stigwood Organisation. At 10 o'clock next morning many of those present at a reception for *Evita* in the Lord Mayor's Parlour at the Adelaide Town Hall had come straight from the party in their dinner suits.

Fire entrance

In its early days the Festival Theatre was an object of curiosity for all South Australians, not least the gentlemen of the Fire Brigade. Seven of them – one white helmet and six reds – took to holding fire inspections in the dressing rooms at 7.30 at night – inconvenient timing for 8 p.m. show starts. The bare-breasted Senegalese Dancers were blamed for innocently encouraging the habit. In 1974 technical manager Dennis Smith arranged for the male *corps de ballet* of the Australian Ballet to be in various stages of undress for the Brigade's arrival. The boys did the rest. "Ooooh, I do like the one in the white helmet" and "that cute number 93 is for me" have resulted in fire inspections at a more respectable hour ever since.

Wizard tea

When he handed over his role for the Adelaide season of *The Wizard of Oz,* actor John Gaden told his successor Bert Newton, below, that because the Wiz had so little to do in the first half, it was his job to make tea for the cast at interval. Bert bought a silver tea service and set about his task. Even when told of the joke, Bert continued to make the tea, with chocolates and biscuits.

The broth of Rudi

Rudolf Nureyev, below, the greatest single crowd-puller to the Festival Theatre so far, wanted chicken broth before he went on stage for the London Festival Ballet in 1975. Dresser Ciro Cantone rang the Green Room. The chef arrived with the bad news. "I'm sorry Mr Nureyev, we only have beef broth." Rudi wasn't having any of it. "I will not go on without chicken broth." A representative of the Michael Edgley organisation was called to the dressing room. After ten minutes, and with three minutes to the curtain, Nureyev announced: "I shall dance tonight." He was swayed by the promise of a permanent table booking at Lyrics restaurant after every show. Rudi never turned up there, but he danced like a dream. "The best I ever saw him," says Ciro.

HEATHER BLEWETT

Dog bites critic

Peter Goers was the "critic who ate Adelaide". The two worst dishes he tasted at the Festival Theatre were *Footrot Flats* – "that was a dog biting a critic" – and a Debbie Reynolds concert – "she was on Planet X and she sang 'Tammy'." Goers's two best meals were the opera *Voss* at the 1986 Adelaide Festival, and *Evita*. He also has held a place in his heart for the late Peter Allen since he told his audience, "I can't believe I'm something to do in Adelaide on a Monday night." Goers himself has appeared on the Festival Theatre stage, as host of a Morning Melodies concert of *Side by Side by Sondheim*. He now lives in Istanbul, and admits he is sentimental about the Festival Centre: "I think the place has held up very well. In the early years I remember sneaking in through the glass doors of the upper foyer and into the boxes. No one checked for tickets. I got away with it for about three seasons of Australian Opera. Those were the days."

Jerry's nicest girl . . .

Jeannie Little, above, is widely regarded by backstage staff as the nicest performer to have worked at the Festival Theatre. During the musical *Jerry's Girls*, Jeannie thanked the cleaners of her Number One Dressing Room every day.

. . . and Joan too

Along with Jeannie is Joan. Dame Joan Sutherland was just as popular behind the scenes. In 1979, while performing in *The Merry Widow* with Australian Opera, she was the mystery guest and prize-giver at the annual Festival Centre Bottom of the River Boat Race on the Torrens. Dame Joan also was a regular in the Green Room. It took a brave diva to dine there in those days. Dame Joan would sup better in the Green Room now, and is always welcome back.

CHAPTER 12

Mr Earle, Birdy and Robbo

Kevin Earle was a gifted accountant bewitched by show business. Tony Frewin was a creature of the theatre, regarded to this day as one of the most imaginative arts marketers Australia has seen. John Robertson was the cool production head, his technical expertise tracing back through the old firm J.C. Williamson's and early Adelaide Festivals.

Between them, from 1979 to 1986 they were responsible for a golden age of the Australian musical stage. The Adelaide Festival Centre Trust, its entrepreneurial fund topped up by *Evita*, led the way in bringing the big shows to Australia.

The musicals were international, the productions were Australian, usually initiated by the Trust and built by the Trust. Earle made the approaches to the owners of the rights, raised the money from co-producers and managed the contracts. Robertson oversaw the productions from conception to opening night and on tour.

Frewin sold the shows to everyone he could.

They filled the void left by the demise of Williamson's in 1976. Their successes attracted the attention of Andrew Lloyd Webber and Cameron Mackintosh. The Centre's expertise, from workshop to box office, impressed entrepreneurs around the world.

Earle preferred to be known as "Mr Earle" by his staff in public. Previously an accountant at Channel 10, he lacked the people skills and charisma of his predecessor Anthony Steel. His shyness was often mistaken for aloofness by his junior staff, who were angered when he ignored them. Those close to him say he was lost in thought, and many of the stars he engaged liked him. Reg Livermore found him "a lovely bear, sweet natured".

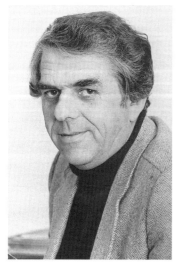

Frewin was known as "Birdy" because of his constant motion. He was head-hunted from Australian Opera and gave the rest of his life to the Festival Centre. Frewin was capable of great exhilaration, great temper and great depression. He was also capable of sweeping the entire Centre along with his enthusiasm. In short, Frewin loved the product he sold – any show, big or small, good or bad.

Robertson was plain "Robbo". As the only one of the three still alive, he takes up the story:

"Kevin had a genius for figures. He would say we can afford to do this, or we can't afford to do that. He knew he had an obligation to run the Centre as efficiently as possible. He also knew we had the facilities and the talent within the organisation to produce a commercial product. He identified the Christmas spot as a revenue-raiser that would be the beginning of a touring circuit. We had the resources to put money back into the Trust.

"Tony was in the forefront of arts marketing in Australia. His ability to present a show to the public is reflected in the way other large theatrical organisations such as Cameron Mackintosh market their product today."

Tony Frewin took his own life in December 1981, too young at 44. "He was a great loss to the Centre and to Australian theatre," says Len Amadio, the former head of the South Australian Department for the Arts. "No one in Australia had quite his breadth of experience. We haven't seen his like since."

Earle and Robertson continued to produce the musicals described in the following chapter. When he had a heart bypass and was told to slow down, Earle replied that he wouldn't. "I love what I'm doing. I'd rather die doing it than sit around with my feet up."

By 1984, Earle was getting home from work around sun-up. That was the year of *Cats*, which would put the Festival Centre on the map as Australia's leading and most complete production house. *Cats* wouldn't have happened without Earle. Nobody else wanted to take the risk. After exhausting every other avenue Earle raised the money from a New Zealand bank.

Cats toured Australia for five years. When it opened in Sydney in July 1985, there was nothing theatrical in Australia the Festival Centre couldn't do. But Earle was gone from the centre by then.

THE ADVERTISER

Above: Tony Frewin – "a creature of the theatre" with Anthony Steel

Left: Kevin Earle – "a genius for figures".

Above: John Robertson – "wonderful time"

The most bitter and personal feud in the Centre's 11 working years had taken its toll. Earle had become a total workaholic, obsessed with the Trust's entrepreneurial activities. The musicals *Song and Dance* and *Oliver!* lost money. Disappointing seasons outside Adelaide left the Trust in financial strife.

Communication and leadership broke down. Younger staff members complained they had nowhere to go in their careers. While Earle had loyal supporters within, the Trust began to feel it was operating in a vacuum.

In late 1984 Earle was offered the chance to resign as general manager. It was a savage irony, because in 1977 Earle and Frewin had put the squeeze on Anthony Steel. Earle accepted the offer, and was replaced by Murray Edmonds, who in his eleven months at the Centre was largely concerned with management–staff relations.

But in the process, the Trust's entrepreneurial activities began to lose their impetus. "When Kevin left the downhill run began, and that was a great tragedy," says Robertson. *Cats* went on to make so much money that, in a period of funding cutbacks, the State Government considered taking those profits away from the Trust.

Instead it allowed the creation of a risk reserve, the first official Government recognition of the Trust's large-scale production ventures.

Earle went into partnership with the former Festival Centre head mechanist Mort Clark to produce the Australian tour of *Starlight Express* from his office in his family home at Moonta. He died in Sydney in November 1989, aged 51, before the opening of his second production, *Chess*.

"People had doubts about Kevin's management style," says John Robertson, "but there is no doubt he raised the profile of the Festival Centre in Australia and overseas. Kevin was very proud of the Dry Creek workshop. Without it the Centre wouldn't be where it is today.

"The musicals were a golden era that didn't end until after *Guys and Dolls* in 1986. Adelaide built shows and toured Australia with them. It was a wonderful time for people who worked on them, and it was a wonderful time for Adelaide."

CHAPTER 13

The Golden Age of Musicals 1980–1986

From 1980 to 1986 the Adelaide Festival Centre Trust dominated the Australian musical stage. It built, produced or co-presented eight major musicals and began relationships with the Really Useful and Cameron Macintosh organisations that continue today.

1980 – EVITA. With Robert Stigwood in association with David Land, the Gwen Burrows Organisation and Michael Edgley International. Jennifer Murphy, John O'May, Peter Carroll, Tony Alvarez.

Critical choice

Audiences loved to see Reg Livermore fall off the tightrope in *Barnum*, because they knew they would love it even more when he got back on and made it to the other side. Which he always did. After writing, designing and directing *Ned Kelly*, Livermore was philosophical when he returned to the Festival Theatre as an actor only in *Barnum*. In the Green Room after the opening he had forgotten his glasses, so a Centre staff member read aloud the local critic's notice to him. "Thank you," Livermore said. "That was very nice. Now will someone else please read me the WHOLE REVIEW?"

1982 – BARNUM.
With Michael Edgley International and the Australian Elizabethan Theatre Trust. Reg Livermore, Gaye MacFarlane.

Left and below: 1982 – OKLAHOMA! With the MLC Theatre Royal and Michael Edgley International. John Diedrich, Henry Szeps, Donna Lee, Sally Butterfield.

The huge stage cloth painted with the famous mountains of *The Sound of Music* became stuck as it was flown in one night. Festival Theatre stagehands worked to free it. At the moment Penelope Richards, as the Countess, said "What I like about you, Captain, is you're as steady as those mountains," those Austrian mountains shook like a Los Angeles earthquake. Bartholomew John, as von Trapp, nearly died of embarrassment. So did the audience, laughing.

1983 – THE SOUND OF MUSIC.
With the Australian Elizabethan Theatre Trust and Michael Edgley International.
Julie Anthony, Bartholomew John.

60

CHAPTER 14

Dunstan's Playhouse papered with people

The Festival Theatre would be, at its best, all things for all people. From its earliest days the theatre was a shared vision, a joint effort by South Australia's political and civic decision-makers, arts leaders, architects, builders, engineers, technicians, its future players and its potential audience.

Everybody, including Don Dunstan, agreed on that. The Playhouse would be for all South Australians too. But the Playhouse would be Dunstan's special pride because it was his special passion. The previous Hall Liberal Government wasn't keen to proceed with the Drama Complex, the recommended Stage Two of the Adelaide Festival Centre.

In plain fact agreed by arts and political observers of the time, without Don Dunstan it is unlikely the Playhouse, the Space and the Amphitheatre would exist today.

Right: The Playhouse: a special passion.

Coathanger City to coathanger

Helmut Bakaitis, George Ogilvie and Rodney Fisher, left, set out from Sydney for their Promised Land called the Playhouse in a green Fiat Bambino known as "the lettuce leaf". Only 160 kilometres from Adelaide the bottom fell out of the tiny car. Fisher concedes that few people will believe him, but he found a coathanger by the side of the road and tied the "lettuce leaf" back together. "Don't ask me how I did it because I still don't know," he says, "but when we arrived Adelaide looked like Florence to me, and it still does."

During research for *By Popular Demand*, Dunstan described the Festival Theatre as "a triumph" for all involved. For the Playhouse he had no words of his own. He quoted the architect Roy Grounds, who was in the throes of designing the Victorian Arts Centre.

Grounds approached the Premier on the opening night of the Playhouse, on 26 October 1974. "He had tears in his eyes," Dunstan recalls. "He was a theatre buff. He said, 'If I can come up with anything near as good in Melbourne as your Playhouse, I will be a proud man'."

More than two decades later, Dunstan was visibly affected in the retelling of the tale and the memory of the night.

According to Peter Ward, author of *A Singular Act – Twenty Five Years of the State Theatre Company of South Australia* and once the Premier's executive assistant, Dunstan had grown up in a local amateur theatre movement deeply influenced by director Colin Ballantyne and his dream of a national theatre of Australia.

In the 1950s the Federal politicians didn't want a national theatre. They gave Australia the Elizabethan Theatre Trust instead. In 1972, at the height of his political dominance of the State and with his artistic authority beyond challenge, Dunstan created the then South Australian Theatre Company as a statutory body, made Ballantyne its chairman, and pledged the unbuilt Playhouse as its permanent home.

Last order

Don Dunstan thought so highly of Colin Ballantyne that he made his mentor a Companion of the Order of St Michael and St George in 1971. Ballantyne's award was the highest imperial honour recommended by the Dunstan Government, and the last by a Labor Government in South Australia.

First-class Humphries

The Performing Arts Collection of South Australia grew out of Don Dunstan's concern for the State's disappearing performing arts heritage. Originally under the aegis of Colin Ballantyne and the State Theatre Company, the Collection transferred to the Trust in 1985. One of its early exhibitions was *The Fashion Diary of a Victorian Housewife – Dame Edna's Wardrobe 1956–1984*, for which Barry Humphries, far right, flew in from Sydney to unpack his cossies. The PAC sent him his airline ticket – first-class, of course, for a big international star. When Humphries arrived from Sydney he told PAC curator Jo Peoples: "I've never flown first-class in my life before, thank you very much."

He didn't stop there. Architect Colin Hassell recalls that the Premier was heavily involved in every aspect of construction of the Playhouse, still officially known along with the Space and the Amphitheatre as the Drama Complex. "The Premier consulted with the builders throughout," Hassell says. "He kept the money coming. He even helped solve the problems of car parking and traffic flow."

In 1972 Britain's Prospect Theatre Company came to the Adelaide Festival. Theatre consultant Tom Brown had designed an open-stage, stalls-only theatre. Dunstan wasn't completely convinced. He showed the plans to the Prospect director Iain Mackintosh, an expert on stage ergonomics.

"Paper the walls with people," Dunstan was told. "Wrap it around with balconies, reduce the distance between the audience and the stage." Brown was persuaded to add the galleries. "That's why the Playhouse remains one of the most workable, playable theatres around," Dunstan says.

The life of the Playhouse began with George Ogilvie's SATC production of *The Three Cuckolds* after a blank verse introduction written by Ward for Dunstan. At the request of Ballantyne, the Chief Justice, John Bray, provided a poem – the traditional prologue for a new theatre.

Rodney Fisher, the present STC artistic director, was in the audience that night. "It was a lovely moment I shall always remember," Fisher says. "When Don Dunstan stood in the centre of prompt side, there was a tremendous feeling of his truly being the person of vision who made the Playhouse happen, and with such speed.

"Dunstan's ability to engender in people the sense of Adelaide as an important centre of the arts was tangible there on the stage."

The great and otherwise moments on that stage are in Peter Ward's book about its resident theatre company. In 1999, the Playhouse, now known as the Optima Playhouse, celebrates its quarter-century too. Fisher, along with members of the original artistic team at the Playhouse 24 years ago, George Ogilvie and Helmut Bakaitis, is already planning the party.

By that day in October 1999, Fisher wants to improve the theatre's sightlines further, and provide better facilities for disabled people. Even without those improvements, Fisher says, "the Playhouse remains one of everyone's favourite theatres, the envy of our profession.

"In the middle of a large performing arts complex it gives a real sense of community. The Playhouse was a wonderful drama theatre when it opened and it is still well thought of today."

It can also be well thought of as Dunstan's Playhouse.

Pointing to Percy

After the last Adelaide performance of his *Tears Before Bedtime*, Humphries filled the boot of his rental car with gladioli. Supper with Jo Peoples and the critic Peter Goers followed, and at 1 a.m. Humphries announced he wished to visit the grave of the composer Percy Grainger, whom he had met as a young man. Peoples drove the rental car into the blackness of West Terrace Cemetery, Goers went in search of Percy, and Humphries pointed. "I think that's Percy's plinth over there!" It was. "We unloaded a boot-full of gladdies onto the grave, said hello to Percy, and left," says Peoples. "It's one of the funniest nights I've ever had. I was sure we would be arrested."

Left: Barry Humphries – "thank you very much"

CHAPTER 15

Small space, large bonus

Hamlet's hundred

In 1995 Richard Roxburgh brought new meaning to "break a leg", the theatrical expression of good luck, during his 100th performance of *Hamlet* for Belvoir Street's Company B in the Space. Roxburgh lunged with his dagger at Peter Carroll as Polonius and slipped, badly injuring his knee. Gillian Jones, playing Gertrude, carried Roxburgh from the stage. After an interval Geoffrey Rush, as Horatio, told the audience it was an early good night from his sweet prince, because by Act V Hamlet was in hospital.

Critical change

Tessa Bremner, then Mrs Anthony Steel, danced a masked duet with Roger Pahl in *Tancred and Clorinda* for the first half of opening night of the Space. Then she made a quick change back into her first-night dress and joined the official guests in the interval, only to be asked, "What did you think of the two dancers, Mrs Steel?" Tessa replied, "Oh they were absolutely marvellous," without missing a beat.

In the 1970s performing arts complexes were all the rage around the Western world. The formula was straightforward and rarely digressed from:

- One lyric theatre
- One concert hall
- One drama theatre
- One experimental theatre

Only a few arts centres combined their lyric theatres and concert halls as the Festival Centre did, but the experimental theatre, the stand-alone "black box", was particularly fashionable then.

So Adelaide got one – the Space.

What Adelaide didn't have, or get, was an experimental theatre company. Nor, when New Opera SA opened the Space on 28 October, 1974, with *Tancred and Clorinda* and 1998 and 2000 Adelaide Festival director Robyn Archer in *The Seven Deadly Sins* did the Trust have an artistic policy for the venue, or any idea how it was going to pay for itself.

Ever since, these deficiencies have caused no end of problems for the versatile little 300-seater hidden away between the Festival Theatre and the Playhouse behind the Amphitheatre. It's too small to make money; if the Trust charged full rental, no company could afford to use it.

The theatre seat subsidy for performances at the Space is greater than the subsidies for the Festival Theatre, the Playhouse and Her Majesty's combined. Finding the right product for the Space has been a challenge for the Trust's programming department for 24 years.

Yet despite its drawbacks the Space has managed to win the affections of both artists and audiences. It is suited to small modern dance performances and cabaret. Touring companies experienced in experimental theatre often bring it to life with stunning impact, notably during Adelaide Festivals.

The Polish company Cricot II's *The Dead Class* in the Space at the 1978

Festival is regarded as not only one of the highlights of any Festival, but as a standout among any productions in the Festival Centre's history. Neil Armfield's promenade production of the Australian musical *Jonah* for the State Theatre Company in 1991 used the venue to full effect by including the audience on the stage and in the action.

The Space is sometimes down, but never out. State Theatre Company artistic director Rodney Fisher has commented on the huge Shakespeare revival taking place at the end of the 20th century. "The question now is whether to maximise the scale of productions of Shakespeare, or go to something more intimate," Fisher says. "The Space is ideal for smaller Shakespeare."

It is also ideal for smaller children. The Space is where many young South Australians have their initial experience of live theatre, with the "Something on Saturday" seasons, school holiday shows, and school productions. For children, the Space is often the first place, and that is its unsung success.

While the theatrical trend of the times dictated that the Space would always happen, the Amphitheatre really did just happen. The lie of the land dictated it. Early in the Centre's construction, it was apparent that the enormous height of

Two-hander

Two Festival Centre staff had formed a relationship. Like all relationships, it had its ups and downs. The couple chose the empty Space to have a blazing argument. Into the middle of it walked a party of tourists led by the Centre's tourist officer Jillian Scott. "Is this a rehearsal?" asked one tourist. "Yes, we must leave immediately," Jillian replied. "Must be that *Who's Afraid of Virginia Woolf?*" said another tourist.

Below: The Space in the round

Above: *The Dead Class* – a stand out
among the best

Right: The Amphitheatre – a
community asset

the Festival Theatre's flytower allied to the natural gentle slope to the Torrens
bank would create a perfect spot for an open-air venue.

The architects and builders put the idea to the State Government. "Well
while you're there design and build an amphitheatre," they were told. The
first performance in the 1200-seat Festival Centre Amphitheatre on Sunday
27 October 1974 was an eight-hour concert featuring Johnny Farnham, Julie
Anthony, Bev Harrell, Wally Carr and compere Bob Francis.

Like the Space, the Amphitheatre is a community asset, as a venue for the
Centre's youth, education and outdoor programs. And again like the Space, the
Amphitheatre comes alive at Festival time.

CHAPTER 16

A big hot deck and an enormous gift

If the Festival Centre was to be an international performing arts complex for music, theatre and opera, its public art would be international too. The Trust, chaired by John Baily, the director of the Art Gallery of South Australia, decided that, and the Premier Don Dunstan agreed.

"As long as the costing is right, it's long been my policy to accept the decisions of my artistic advisers," Dunstan told Baily. "So you decide."

If the Playhouse foyer on the Plaza were to be made next to useless as an entrance by the building of the car parks underneath, the Festival Centre would have a gallery space there that bore no relation to any other gallery in Adelaide at the time. On this occasion Silver Harris, theatre designer, decided that, and general manager Anthony Steel agreed.

"Go on, give it a go," Steel told Harris.

Baily's free hand stirred up the one real controversy in the building of the Festival Centre – the concrete environmental sculpture City Sign, known to all by the surname of its creator, Otto Hajek.

"The Hajek" dominates the Southern Plaza and with a maximum height of 10.6 metres is held to be the largest artwork in Australia. Baily chose the West German artist because his work in integrating art and architecture in public places was internationally recognised at the time.

Using the modernist aesthetic of the Bauhaus, Hajek created site-specific monumental pieces aimed to humanise their inner urban surroundings. To this day his critics claim that in Adelaide Hajek got it the other way around.

"The problem we faced was that if the huge deck of the Plaza was left unrelieved it would've been like a desert, especially in Adelaide's hot weather," Baily says. "I had seen examples of Hajek's work, and he seemed at the time to be the answer to that big hot deck."

From the beginning of the search for a centrepiece for the Plaza, South Australian artists lobbied for the commission. When Hajek's name was

Above: Otto Hajek

Left: City Sign – "a piece of South Australian history"

Cool solution

Otto Hajek's skill was working with architects. He excelled with Hassell and Partners. City Sign camouflages the Festival Centre's main cooling tower.

Silver Harris's views on the "Hajek" in this chapter are in the past tense. Why? The integrity and appropriateness of the sculpture to the site were obviously misunderstood by many, she says, including those who authorised the "treeing" of the Festival Centre. Consequently many of the Hajek surfaces were removed. "What is left is only part of the original. A commission can be accepted or rejected, but I don't believe it can be tampered with."

Right: "An expression of the time it was built . . ."

announced there was further controversy. Dunstan held a symposium in the Space. When the Queen opened the Plaza and City Sign at the Festival Centre completion ceremony in March 1977, a group of artists protested.

But the "Hajek" was here to stay. Dunstan defends it: "It's a piece of South Australian history. There might be a few things Hajek ignored, such as the harshness of the Australian sun and more particularly the light. He might have done something to provide more shade and relief from the glare, but as an artistic work it's fine."

John Baily admits there could have been other solutions to the big hot deck, "but they were not easy to arrive at on the Plaza. It didn't lend itself to the planting of trees. Like the Centre itself, I believe the Hajek belongs to its time. It is an expression of the time it was built, and always will be."

Silver Harris says, "Hajek's hard-edged sculptures and Plaza surfaces were a harmonious surround to the beautifully angled shapes of the two major theatre structures. They provided necessary breathing space for such visually significant buildings, and the whole contrasted nicely with the soft lines of the river and its lovely tree plantings and the rather stoic lines of Parliament House and the Railway Station."

Harris should know. She spent 15 years across the Plaza from the Hajek in the Festival Centre Gallery, later the Artspace, fully appreciating the "enormous gift" Steel had given her with his "full support and a sense of respect for putting untried ideas to the test".

She challenged artists to use the daylight, the reflective glass, the unusual shape and the ever-present dynamic of people moving through the Plaza "to reverse the deeply ingrained – at that time rules of 'don't touch' art. The most successful shows were those by artists who understood these challenges and were inspired to stretch themselves for such a rare opportunity with a much more general public than artists were used to."

In keeping with the performing arts nature of the Centre, Harris would often stage the opening of exhibitions, with on one occasion, dancers and tuxedoed waiters leading the crowd up from the Torrens through the Plaza ponds to the show by Margo Lewers. On another, the artist Tineke Adolphus and her family filled the Gallery and the stairway to the Playhouse, drawing theatre patrons to the Gallery while Adolphus's musician husband Paul played Pied Piper.

Second chance

Hajek wasn't John Baily's first choice to solve the Plaza problem. The initial approach was to young South Australian artist Nigel Lendon, now living in Canberra. Lendon decided his stylistic interests lay elsewhere at the time.

Below: "Left unrelieved it would have been like a desert . . ."

"Then there was the time we were rained out trying to cook vegies New Guinea-style in a pit in the park," Harris says, "but nothing could dampen the enthusiasm for the mural being painted inside and the totem pole being carved outside by two young Papua-New Guinea artists." The totem pole, known as the House Post, is on the Festival Centre Terrace.

Fay Bottrell's *Fabrications*, made entirely of ribbons, drew 5735 people to the first exhibition in the Artspace in September and October 1975. That number is exactly 5735 more than would have passed through the doors of the upper Playhouse foyer had Silver Harris not given Anthony Steel something else to think about.

Below: Dame Barbara Hepworth's Ultimate Form – with Lord Mayor Bill Clampett, John Baily and Don Dunstan

In 1998, under director Vivonne Thwaites, the Trust's visual arts program continues to draw crowds to the Artspace and to exhibitions in the Centre's foyers and spaces. In those foyers and spaces, and on the terraces and the Plaza, are the results of the Centre's commissioning and aquisition program begun by the City Council in 1970 and guided in its infancy by John Baily.

All told there are 32 permanent major works in and around the Festival Centre. They are by some of the great names of Australian and international art, among them Sidney Nolan, Fred Williams, Leonard French, Barbara Hepworth, Clifford Frith, John Dowie, Milton Moon, Max Lyle and Bert Flugelman.

The financial worth of the artworks is immeasurable, although that is not the point, says John Baily. "They belong to the building in its many forms. They are there for everyone to enjoy. The Festival Centre would not be the Festival Centre without them."

CHAPTER 17

From shoeboxes to the Best Available Seating System

The first phone call to BASS was a wrong number.

In 1974, for the first Adelaide Festival held in the Festival Centre, all the ticketing was done from Dressing Room Seven.

On the opening night of the Festival Theatre in 1973, the rain leaked through the Plaza into the box office. It took a baby's bath to prevent a flood.

Patti Bennett and Maxine Forrester, the Festival Centre's original "box office girls" in the early 1970s, used shoeboxes to hold the "trips", or ticket stubs. For a big show, one shoebox for each performance. Patti and Max got the boxes from Myer, Johnnies and DJ's.

Above: Patti Bennett – "rapport at the counter"

That was then. Today BASS and the Festival Centre box office is regarded as one of the best and most efficient ticketing agencies in the country. BASS has 38 outlets from Mount Gambier to Roxby Downs, with 150 sales representatives. It sells tickets for almost anything from the Crows and the Power to State Opera and State Theatre Company subscriptions to Michael Jackson and the Therry Society. It has developed Australia's first internet ticketing service.

BASS was Kevin Earle's idea, after he heard about it from Roger Stephens, chief executive of the JFK Centre for the Performing Arts in Washington D.C. Stephens introduced Earle to the concept of a government-subsidised arts centre paying its way by involvement in commercial theatre, which led to the creation of the troubled *Ned Kelly*. Stephens also told Earle about the Bay Area Seating System in San Francisco. Computerised ticketing was the future; in time, the public would find it easier to book for Earle's shows.

Earle, Anthony Steel and Patti Bennett went to the US in 1977 to see it. Bennett was a "hard ticket girl" of the old cinema school, but she had done a crash course in computing before she left. The men flew on to New York to try

Perfect score

The moment every box office person dreams about arrived at the Festival Theatre with *Evita*. Every seat for every show was sold, and not one complimentary ticket was issued. Ah, sheer box office perfection!

H holds on tight

The Earl of Harewood, also known simply as "H", was used to others holding his tickets for him. When he was artistic director of the 1988 Festival, Lord Harewood was left to his own devices. "H" kept losing his tickets. BASS's Maxine Forrester had to organise yet another batch of replacements. "You'd think His Lordship could hold on to his tickets for 20 minutes," she told a booking clerk. Behind her a voice was heard. "Madam, I shall try. I shall try very hard."

Desert b✳✳✳ing

BASS Online's Most Remote Customer Award so far goes to geophysicist Peter Harvey, of Morphettville. Peter won the prestigious virtual trophy in September 1997 when he booked four tickets for *Shopping and F✳✳✳ing* at the Playhouse from a seismic exploration camp in the Western Desert of Egypt. Peter used the Intelsat satellite system, and the Festival Centre's information systems manager Peter Barnes clinched the deal at his workstation in Adelaide. "Certainly beats carrier pigeons," Desert Peter e-mailed Centre Peter, and later he used the same method to book for Twyla Tharp.

to persuade the choreographer Twyla Tharp to come to the 1978 Festival, leaving Bennett in Oakland, California, with Steel's words "You're in the job because you have the expertise. You look after it." Bennett spent three weeks learning the Bay Area system. She returned to Adelaide confident that it would make a contribution to the business of the Festival Centre. Bennett recalls that the Trustee David Bright had a knowledge of computing and was keen to see BASS on line.

"Bay Area" became "Best Available". BASS made its debut at the 1978 Festival, the first time the system had been outside North America. The public was still so wary of it that for the first 12 months, the box office kept the old-fashioned "maps", or seating plans, on the front counter. "People thought if they weren't marked off on the map, they wouldn't get their seats," Bennett says.

"And for the public we had a little calculator on hand to work out the cost of their tickets, even though the computers did it for us."

BASS had early problems. The system had difficulty with large subscription seasons such as opera, suffered all the usual software and hardware breakdowns, and consumed valuable office space in the Centre at an alarming rate.

Now BASS has a staff of 66, 50 terminals and 25 phone lines in the old rehearsal room under the Southern Plaza. As well as selling tickets on the internet, it may soon be linked to other systems around the country.

It's all computerised now, but there is still room for the human element at the box office. "When you work there you have to like people," says Patti Bennett, the Trust's box office manager from 1971 to 1990. "You like the rapport with them at the counter, talking to them on the phone, looking after the venues and promoting the shows.

"People buy a ticket. That's the start. They go to a show and see it. That's the finish. The transaction is complete. At the box office we always get a sense of satisfaction in that."

Hard ticketing, modern style

Until last year, the Festival Theatre's seating was arranged in the European manner – 1-3-5-7-9 from one side of the auditorium, and 2-4-6-8-10 from the other. When *Cats* came to Adelaide in 1989, a woman made a group booking for 400 seats. Lorraine Douglas, now BASS's group sales manager, bundled up the tickets and sent them off. The woman phoned her next day. "Why did you do this to me? Why did you split up the seats? I've been up all night putting them back in numerical order. I am devastated." The woman obviously had never been to the Festival Theatre before. Lorraine sent a courier, and fixed the problem. For *The Phantom of the Opera*, Cameron Macintosh cried "enough", and the Festival Theatre's seats now are numbered 1-2-3-4-5-6-7-8-9-10.

Far left: "The Ladies" at the box office, hard tickets time

Left: Best Available Seating System for a Prince

CHAPTER 18

The King and I – Broadway bound, and much more

Shall We Dance in Oregon?

The Trust's *The King and I* rolled on in the US in 1998 with a touring version starring Hayley Mills and later Marie Osmond. On the 25th anniversary of the Adelaide Festival Centre, Anna and her King of Siam danced in Portland, Oregon.

The King and I was but a few days away from never making it to the Festival Theatre stage.

Trust construction manager Ron Wood told general manager Tim McFarlane and program director Rob Brookman that unless he could start ordering materials immediately, he could not build the show in time for its scheduled June 1991 opening.

This was January, and *The King and I* had to be opulent, exotic, gorgeous and glamorous. Shows like that don't come together overnight. At a conservative estimate, this one was three months behind. Not much more money was needed, but no private investor would give it.

It was almost too late. Cancellation was the likeliest option. McFarlane had one last pitch. In Brookman's office one night, he tried it. The money came through, from a private investor in Sydney. "Now we can do *The King and I* – and we will do it in four months!" McFarlane rejoiced.

And they did.

Five years later in New York the Adelaide Festival Centre Trust/Gordon Frost Attractions production of *The King and I* won four Tonys – Broadway's equivalent of the Oscars – before a television audience of hundreds of millions. The show was judged best revival of a musical. Brian Thomson won best set design and Roger Kirk best costume design. Donna Murphy, who replaced Hayley Mills as Anna Leonowens in New York, was named best actress in a musical.

By happy coincidence Rob Brookman collected the Trust's Tony on 2 June 1996, 23 years to the day after the Festival Theatre opened.

The King and I finished its run of 773 performances at the Neil Simon Theatre in February 1998. It was the 10th longest running revival of a musical in Broadway history, and it justified the decision of Mary Rodgers, daughter of the composer Richard, that "if we ever do another revival of *The King and I* on Broadway, it will be this one".

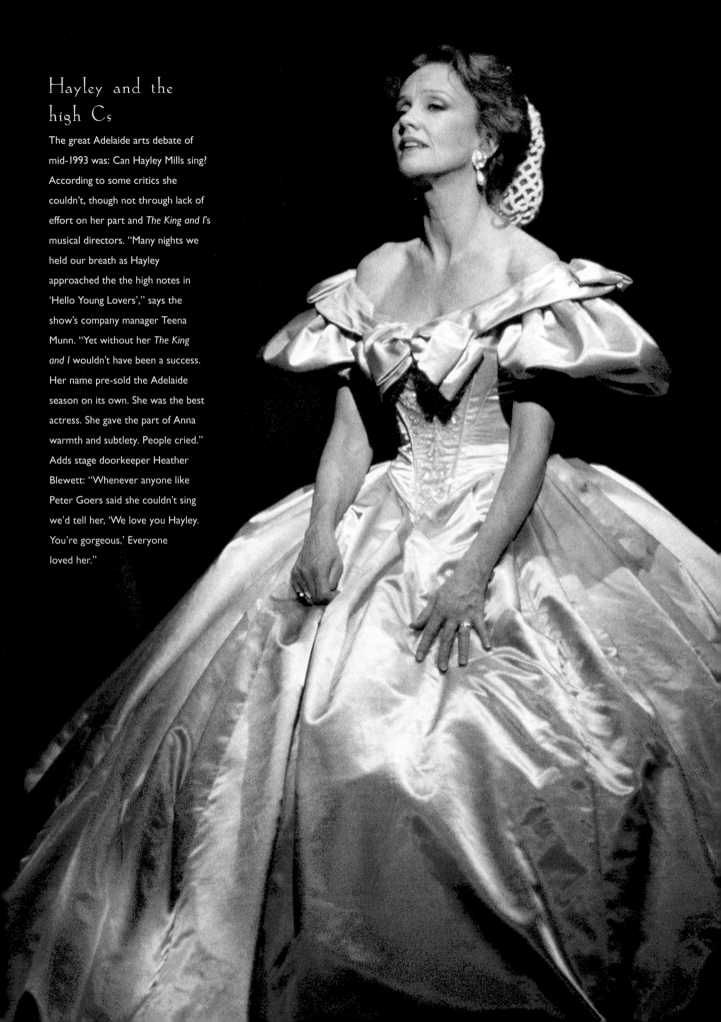

Hayley and the high Cs

The great Adelaide arts debate of mid-1993 was: Can Hayley Mills sing? According to some critics she couldn't, though not through lack of effort on her part and *The King and I*'s musical directors. "Many nights we held our breath as Hayley approached the the high notes in 'Hello Young Lovers'," says the show's company manager Teena Munn. "Yet without her *The King and I* wouldn't have been a success. Her name pre-sold the Adelaide season on its own. She was the best actress. She gave the part of Anna warmth and subtlety. People cried." Adds stage doorkeeper Heather Blewett: "Whenever anyone like Peter Goers said she couldn't sing we'd tell her, 'We love you Hayley. You're gorgeous.' Everyone loved her."

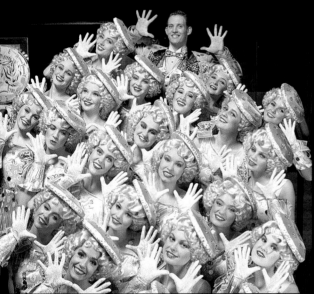

Opposite page:
1988 – *MY FAIR LADY*.
With Victoria State Opera. Helen Buday,
June Bronhill, Simon Gallaher, John
Waters, Noel Ferrier.

Top and top right:
1990 – *BIG RIVER*.
With Essington Entertainment and the
Gordon/Frost Organisation. Cameron
Daddo, Doug Parkinson, Marcia Hines,
Bruce Spence, Edwin Hodgeman.

Above and left:
1993 – *42nd Street*.
With Helen Montagu in association with
David Merrick. Nancye Hayes, William
Zappa, Toni Lamond, Leonie Page.

Right: 1991 – *THE KING AND I*.
With Gordon/Frost Attractions. Hayley
Mills, Tony Marinyo, William Zappa.

Above: 1996 – *The King and I* opens on
Broadway with Lou Diamond Phillips
and Donna Murphy in the lead roles.

Above: 1993 – *SOUTH PACIFIC*.
With Gordon/Frost Attractions. Paige
O'Hara, Andre Jobin, Philip Gould, Paul
Blackwell, Ros Ryan.

Left: 1994 – *ME AND MY GIRL*.
With Jon Nicholls and the Queensland
Performing Arts Trust by arrangement
with the Noel Gay Organisation. Derek
Metzger, Rachael Beck, Peter Whitford,
Edwin Hodgeman.

1996 – *CRAZY FOR YOU*.
With John Frost and Phillip Emanuel.
Georgie Parker, Jim Walton.

Above and below:
1995 – HELLO DOLLY.
With John Frost. Jill Perryman, Ron
Haddrick, Jackie Love, Jeremy Stanford.

Above: 1996 – Philippe Genty's *Stowaways*.

Left: 1991 – Philippe Genty's *Desirs Parade*.

Below: 1997 – Womadelaide.

Had the Trust not received that endorsement from the Rodgers and Hammerstein office, *The King and I* probably would've ended up at Wingfield Dump, says Brookman. Instead it became the first Australian musical production to make it on Broadway.

The King and I was the centrepiece of the Trust's second golden age of musicals, begun tentatively but successfully with *My Fair Lady* in 1988. After hard financial times and with the State Government on their tail, McFarlane and Brookman realised the Trust had two choices: either retreat further, or go again with the skills it knew it possessed to create profits through musical productions.

McFarlane sold the politicians a vision of gradually decreasing Government support through those profits, and Brookman produced the program. "What seemed absolutely clear was that a major capital city arts centre like ours should aspire to this level of activity," Brookman says.

"Our philosophy was that the musicals would meet three needs. They would provide theatre usage, satisfy audience demand and generate funds for our core program activities – non-musical productions and events of high artistic quality that would meet the Trust's artistic objectives but might never make a profit."

Other Australian arts centres felt similarly. They faced an intermittent and unreliable supply of musical theatre. The Trust was instrumental in using the Confederation of Australian Performing Arts Centres, formed in the early 1970s, to create a structure in which each city would share pre-production costs proportionate to the number of performances in its venue.

Each of the cities then took responsibility for its own seasons of *The King and I*, *42nd Street*, *South Pacific*, *Me and My Girl* and *Hello Dolly*. In Sydney, without a performing arts centre venue, the CAPAC members shared the risk.

During negotiations for *Big River* a relationship developed between the Trust and former Adelaide man John Frost, of the Gordon/Frost Organisation in Sydney. Frost, once an usher at Her Majesty's, suggested *The King and I* as a co-production and the link between the Trust and him continued through to 1998 with *Crazy for You*.

All but two of the musicals in the Adelaide Festival Centre Trust's second golden era made profits of varying sizes. They had export value too; along with *The King and I* to the United States, *South Pacific* toured to Thailand and Hong Kong, and *Me and My Girl* and *42nd Street* to New Zealand.

Most importantly though, the musicals kept the Festival Theatre and other venues around Australia from going dark, entertained many thousands of patrons and provided the foundation for an imaginative programming schedule

Me and My Knickers

As Sally Smith, Rachael Beck wore red frilly lace panties under her red silk chiffon dress for the falling in love dance sequence in *Me and My Girl*. One night the elastic broke as she completed a twirl. Cool as you like, Rachel stepped out of her knickers, picked them up with her big toe, kicked them in the air, caught them, and tossed them into the wings. "Utterly professional," says Trust production manager Ken Wilby, still lost in admiration. "Lucky she didn't have to do another twirl though."

When rain from the Cyclone Bobby depression flooded the Nullarbor Plain in 1995, the Trust's tour of the Royal National Theatre's *An Inspector Calls,* right, came to a soggy halt at Kalgoorlie Railway Station. For almost a week the Trust tried to get the set to Sydney in time for its final Australian date. Army and Air Force Hercules and air freighters from as far away as Hong Kong were canvassed, all to no avail. Then Australian Air Express told Trust production manager Ken Wilby that a DC8 rented for a Janet Jackson tour was available for a day. The crew of His Majesty's in Perth loaded the plane, but the crew of Her Majesty's in Sydney had taken the night off for the Gay Mardi Gras. The Trust lost five performances of *An Inspector Calls* but finished with a sell-out season. "It was an incredible week," says Wilby, "and I still say it was an ex-CIA plane." For the record Roger Chapman, former Magpie and Carclew director and later RNT touring manager, had told the company before it left England that "the Nullarbor never floods".

that made the Trust not only the busiest producer in Australia, but also the most active presenter.

Mounting new productions and presenting events other than musicals was the flip-side of the Centre's more flamboyant activities. Funding the art with commercial work in the face of dwindling public subsidies was the primary objective of the second golden era. In the first, the big stage musicals were the beginning, middle and end.

When some of them lost money Kevin Earle was hard-pressed to explain why he had taken the commercial risks, because he was unable to point to any

successful non-musical productions that might have grown out of the profits of moneyspinners such as *Evita*.

In the second golden era the hard-earned musical dollar has gone further. It has been the financial springboard for the Trust's Brave New Works theatre program, holiday seasons for young people, cabaret, World Theatre and Made to Move seasons, *The Advertiser* Summer Season, free winter and summer concert series and one-offs such as *Porgy and Bess* at the Trust-managed Her Majesty's Theatre.

About half of the shows in the Festival Centre are actively presented by the Trust. It has co-produced new work with local companies such as Patch Theatre and Vital Statistix, and was a regular partner with the now defunct Red Shed.

Orchestras toured in conjunction with the Trust have included the Czech Philharmonic, the National Symphony of the Ukraine and the Stuttgart Chamber Orchestra with the Prague Chamber Choir. The Trust has a special relationship with France's Philippe Genty, with four tours from 1989 making a total of seven since the company first appeared at the 1978 Adelaide Festival.

Artistic and commercial objectives also would occasionally dovetail, as in the case of Genty's only show produced outside France. *Stowaways* was created in Adelaide, produced by the Trust and toured around Australia and France in 1996.

And then there is WOMADELAIDE, the world music festival that made its Australian debut at Brookman's 1992 Festival, and with three more since, has become South Australia's second major popular performance event.

The expansion of the Trust's entrepreneurial activities also included touring of existing shows. The 1995 visit of Britain's Royal National Theatre Company with *An Inspector Calls* was one the most prestigious and successful Australian tours mounted by the Trust, and was followed in 1997 by a 13-week tour by the Royal Shakespeare Company. The diversification also led to the Trust producing the first Madame Tussaud's exhibition held outside London, in Melbourne in 1997.

In 1998, with the mega-musicals such as *The Phantom of the Opera* and even the big musicals such as *The King and I* possibly priced into the past, the first Australian musical production on Broadway, with four Tonys to boot, is a hard act to follow. But the Festival Centre Trust is pledged to doing so with innovative and diverse programming into the 21st century.

Above: Khun Knit Kounavudhi, Rob Brookman and Khun Suchai Kenkarnkar with a model of *South Pacific*

CHAPTER 19

The best address:
Sunset Boulevard, Dry Creek

You want to put on a big show.

Where do you start?

You start with the Adelaide Festival Centre Trust, at Dry Creek, where the big shows have had their beginnings for the past 15 years.

In the early eighties *Evita* had its beginning at Mile End in a dirt-floored railway shed. *Oklahoma!* was built at Norwood in a gutted cinema that later became the Odeon Theatre. *The Sound of Music*, *Song and Dance*, *Barnum* and *Oliver!* began at Edwardstown in a warehouse opposite Castle Plaza.

Then, in late 1984, came *Cats*. The sheer size of the Lloyd Webber musical demanded a complete fit-up of the set before the show went on the road. The Trust moved its scenery workshop to an old foundry among the factories and warehouses at Dry Creek, north of Adelaide.

The foundry's 10-metre minimum ceiling height accommodated the set. The 2000-square metre floor space made room to build *Cats*. It was the footprint of bigger things to come. Since then Dry Creek has been the birthplace of most Australian productions of the major musicals of the late 20th century.

The Phantom of the Opera, *Sunset Boulevard* and *Les Miserables* were built there. So were *The King and I*, *South Pacific*, *Miss Saigon*, *Hello Dolly*, *Aspects of Love*, *Are You Lonesome Tonight?*, *Joseph and the Amazing Technicolor Dreamcoat*, *The Rocky Horror Show*, *Five Guys Named Mo* along with most of *West Side Story* and *Starlight Express*.

The Trust's Dry Creek workshop, with its smaller version at Hendon, is the foremost theatre scenery construction facility in the Southern Hemisphere and up with the best in the world. It's a well-told story in the industry that when Victorian Premier Jeff Kennett made his takeover bid for the arts around Australia, he gave up when he got to Dry Creek.

This was one Kennett could not have. The international impresarios Andrew Lloyd Webber and Cameron Mackintosh, willing partners with the Trust, liked it

Right: Ron Wood – "We had to go and do it ourselves."

just the way it was, where it was. And why wouldn't they? The Trust is the only organisation in Australia that offers complete workshop services from set-making to hydraulics and automation. It delivers on time and on budget and maintains the shows.

"Dry Creek is one of the jewels in the Festival Centre's crown," says former Trust general manager Tim McFarlane.

In 1980 *Evita* was a "thimble" compared with the mega-musicals *Phantom*, *Saigon* and *Sunset*, says the Trust's scenery construction manager Ron Wood, but it was in the Mile End dirt that the future was decided.

"People in the Trust realised that if the vision of the Centre as an entrepreneur was to survive, we had to go and do it ourselves," Wood says. "Why pay someone else to build *Evita*? It was something special to all of us. The show toured and made a lot of money. *Evita* proved to us that we could do it. It proved to others that we could do it."

The Australian production of *Cats* was final proof to the show-business world of the staging expertise hidden away in Dry Creek. It was the first time hydraulics had been used in a Trust set, and it set scenery mechanics standards maintained today at the nearby Gepps Cross engineering workshop.

Dry Creek does the pretty stuff, Gepps Cross makes it work, says Wood. Mechanical services manager John Mignone, who began as a temporary Trust employee fixing the Centre's air-conditioning, is in charge of development of the latest in computer-driven theatre automation.

Both Trust departments use local materials whenever they can, and in full swing can employ 40 people. Their know-how can have its spin-offs, too; the expertise that went into building and operating the chandelier in *Phantom* was used again on the two atrium chandeliers in Melbourne's Crown Casino.

Since 1980, Festival Centre Trust sets have toured Australia, New Zealand, South-East Asia, South Africa, Germany and Broadway with *The King*

Below: Ten people worked for 12 weeks on the mansion in *Sunset Boulevard*. "This is the biggest individual theatre piece you'll ever build," Ron Wood told them. "This is the ultimate for any scenery builder." The aluminium, plywood and fibreglass mansion cost $500,000.

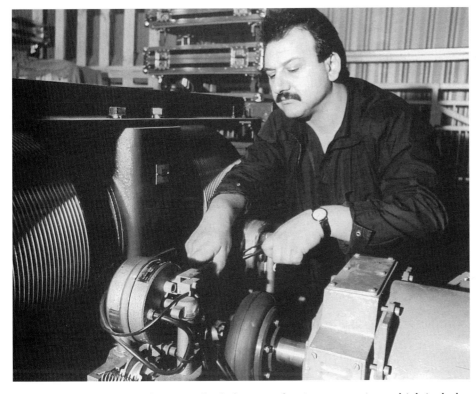

and I. In April 1998, *Show Boat*, built for a production consortium which includes Canada's Livent Inc. and Melbourne entrepreneur David Marriner, opened in Sydney's new Lyric Theatre at Star City.

The success of the Dry Creek workshop is based on its credibility. "Entrepreneurs know they aren't going to the boondocks when they come here," Ron Wood says. "They know that our industry in Adelaide is world-class. It is based on personalities.

"We love the business. You have to, to stay in it. When we're building a show we become one big family."

Show business is also a highly undisciplined industry, says John Mignone. "Where we are in it, we are dealing with a bunch of artistic people who are issuing directions to financial people, and we are taking instructions from financial people.

"But we have to perceive the artistic needs as well."

That is also the beauty of working in one of the best theatre workshops in the world.

The Phantom of Woodville

Old musicals never die, they just come home to rest. As well as building the big ones, Adelaide stores them. Really Useful and Cameron Mackintosh have warehouses at Woodville. In them are *Sunset Boulevard*, *Cats*, *Miss Saigon*, *Five Guys Named Mo* and components of *The Phantom of the Opera*. *Les Miserables* was there too, until it went back on the road. The staff of the Dry Creek workshop put *Les Mis* together again, of course.

Marceau speaks!

The lighting plot called for a blackout in a performance by the great French mime artist Marcel Marceau. All the lights went out, except one. A new stage lighting system had been installed. A dimmer wouldn't dim. Ever the professional, Marceau stayed in his pose. "Turn off that light," he whispered. Nobody could. Eventually Marceau stormed off, and cancelled the show. The only night Marcel Marceau spoke on stage became known as Black Monday in the Festival Theatre.

Billy, we don't want it

The worst recorded audience attendance at a Festival Centre venue is four for *You Want It, Don't You Billy?* at the Space in 1976. Twenty-seven was Billy's top audience figure. One night the company packed up and went home to Melbourne. The Festival Centre backstage staff didn't even know *Billy* had gone.

Prince of Darkness

The Prince of Wales was given a tour of the Festival Centre. As he walked through a door to the Festival Theatre first balcony, the house lights went out. When he arrived at the door on the other side Prince Charles said to usher Mary Pomeroy, "Whew. That was like the Black Hole of Calcutta in there." A republican stage electrician was believed to be the culprit.

Godunov for chooks

Never act with children and animals, W.C. Fields once said. Never sing with chooks, the bass Bruce Martin might have added. Martin sang the part of Varlaam the vagabond in *Boris Godunov* for Australian Opera at the Festival Theatre in November 1980. For atmosphere in Act Two, a dozen hens were required to roost outside an inn. But these chooks were smart. They realised that if they edged towards centre stage as Martin flung open the inn door while singing his toes off, it was too late for anyone to stop them and they could join in too. They screeched and flapped every night. Two flew into the audience, to be retrieved by an apologetic mechanist. Another went for the orchestra pit, alighting on the head of a viola player, who failed to maintain her composure. A net was then strung over the pit, but the chooks continued to squawk along with *Boris*.

OPERA AUSTRALIA

Dame Margot Nagy'd

One of the greatest stars to adorn the Festival Theatre stage was Dame Margot Fonteyn, right. Luminous in her beauty, graceful in the extreme, she danced in *La Sylphide* with Scottish Ballet in 1974. Dame Margot was also very petite, and her premier danseur, Ivan Nagy, was rather larger. Act Two Scene Two called on Nagy, as James, to dance around Dame Margot, as La Sylphide. Then the pair would kiss, and La Sylphide's wings would fall away. This time though Nagy danced straight into his partner, knocking into her and dislodging a wing. Sporting a massive bruise on her shoulder, Dame Margot spun around and pirouetted off stage, where another dancer and a dresser ripped off the other wing. Then she danced back on, grabbed Nagy, put him back into position, and proceeded, with most of the audience none the wiser. To this day, any less-than-dexterous male dancing in the Festival Theatre is known as "doing a Nagy".

Papal performance

The most famous Shoes to have trod the boards of the Festival Theatre are those of the Fisherman. At 8 o'clock on the morning of Sunday 30 November 1986, Pope John Paul II took to the stage to address 2000 farmers and pastoralists of the Rural Australia organisation. His straight man was Federal Minister Ian McLachlan, then president of the National Farmers' Federation. Afterwards, outside the Festival Centre, the Pope met Melinda, his first baby kangaroo.

THE ADVERTISER

CHAPTER 20

Mr Pullen and the Tinsel Department

Above: Mr Pullen

Right: With his toffee apples

Far right: Impeccable presentation

The American rock legend Dr Hook boogied well past his young audience's bedtime at the Festival Theatre in 1977. Anxious parents of teenagers milled in the foyer complaining to front-of-house manager George Pullen.

Pullen threatened to unplug the group's amplifiers. Dr Hook's roadies told him he would face a serious damage bill if he did. The band played on. The next night Pullen placed a dozen bottles of Southern Comfort on every available flat surface on the stage.

The band became so mellow the show was over by 10.

That was the late George Edward Pullen at work. As the plaque outside the Festival Theatre foyer says, he was "theatres manager of the Adelaide Festival Centre Trust from the commencement of operations on 9 April 1973 until 10 March 1989". The plaque is "In recognition of his dedicated service to the performing arts and the Adelaide Festival Centre".

Pullen was a master of the world of front-of-house, a charming, consummate servant of the theatre customer long before the term "customer service" was invented. Trained by J.C. Williamson's and on the Australian cinema circuit, he called his staff the Tinsel Department.

Pullen believed the Tinsel Department should be human, not mechanical, and much more than ticket-to-seat. The ushers were there to provide a friendly welcome, and to be genial, knowledgeable hosts. Like tinsel on a Christmas tree, they enhanced the theatre-going experience but were not the whole theatre-going experience.

Like Kevin Earle, Pullen asked his staff to call him "Mr Pullen" in public. Even Mr Earle and Mr Steel and Mr McFarlane called him Mr Pullen. Everyone else was "Mr", "Mrs" or "Miss". The public would be treated the same way – with courtesy, and the public would respond accordingly.

As much as he loved the pomp and ceremony of the grand occasion, Pullen was the first to step forward when the going got too stiff. "He walked through

During the Christmas return season of *Cats* in 1995, a theatregoer in the Bistro, now the Backstage Bar and Grill, told front-of-house staffer Nicholas Bishop she would buy a program from him if he sang for her. Little did she know that Nicholas was a busy singer and actor with the G & S Society and amateur groups. He went down on bended knee and serenaded the woman with "Memory" from *Cats*. Nicholas received a standing ovation from the Bistro crowd, sold all his programs, and is still singing.

the VIP situation with great confidence and aplomb," says John Glennon, Pullen's protege and now the Trust's theatre services manager, "and inspired the rest of us to that level.

"You have to remember that VIPs don't necessarily know what to do in those circumstances. A lot of people stand back. George stepped in and made Governors-General and Governors feel comfortable."

Because of his vast experience in an inexperienced team, Pullen's influence was invaluable throughout the Centre in its earliest days. He organised the tacked-on administration offices as best he could. He ran the Bistro in its formative, happiest times. He designed the front-of-house uniforms, sometimes with Dame Ruby Litchfield.

Pullen made visiting artists feel at home. Everyone in the Australian Opera and Australian Ballet knew him, and he knew them. Coming to Adelaide to see George made the Festival Theatre popular backstage as well as up front.

He didn't wait for memos. When something went wrong, Pullen fixed it. He applied the same speed and purpose to his front-of-house duties. "George never panicked," says Glennon. "One time a woman in the audience took a bad turn. George called for a doctor over the p.a. system.

"Because it was a concert by an international symphony orchestra, there were several doctors in the house. In the foyer George chose a doctor and made sure the ambulance arrived before the end of the show. By the time the audience came out, the woman was safe in hospital."

Pullen's dedication was absolute. He had been on holidays when he read in

The Foyer follies

If there were flaws in George Pullen's otherwise impeccable demeanour, they were a certain old-fashioned view of a woman's role and an inability to foresee the future. Pullen would advertise female ushers' positions as "suitable for single mothers or divorced or separated ladies". During the International Year of Women in 1975, a group of women met in the Playhouse foyer. Pullen found such a gathering on his patch untenable. "Go home and put dresses on," he shouted. "And stay there and have babies." Thirty women chased Pullen through the foyer and into the Playhouse auditorium, where two members of the Tinsel Department slammed the door behind him. Pullen continued to berate the women from the Playhouse VIP gallery. "The women were gunning for him," says theatre services assistant Ciro Cantone. "They almost knocked the door down and climbed up into the gallery. In the end we grabbed him and snuck him to safety through the Playhouse backstage area. George was very lucky he wasn't thrown in the Torrens."

Right: No sour faces

the *Sunday Mail* that an accountants' conference would begin the next day at the Festival Theatre. Pullen realised that none of the Tinsel Department had been rostered for it. The thought of 2000 accountants left unsupervised in his theatre was too much for him. Anything could happen.

He organised for four of his staff and himself to come in on their days off. The accountants went quietly. Problem solved.

In private Pullen was less formal. Theatre life was fun. Front-of-house was in the theatre, so it should be fun. If it was, the fun would flow on to the public. He had pet names for all his ushers, whom he also called his "toffee apples".

An accomplished ballroom dancer, Pullen would waltz a female usher across the foyer. If a "toffee apple" appeared in a bad mood, he would ask, "What's wrong sour face? We can't present that face to our customers. Tell me all about it."

Today the Festival Centre front-of-house numbers 15 permanent staff and 65 casual. George Pullen's old Tinsel Department now also has responsibility for the administration reception area, car parking, cleaning, security, special tours and Her Majesty's Theatre, and hires out its expertise to other theatres.

Even with the added duties "it's not really a job," says John Glennon. "It's more a chronic condition. Once you're exposed to working anywhere in theatre, you go through the looking glass and become part of it for life. George passed on the condition to us in front of house.

"Mr Pullen, that is."

CHAPTER 21

"I still feel the Festival Theatre is part of me"

From the first chairman, John Baily in 1971 to the present chair James Porter in 1998, the Adelaide Festival Centre has had 37 Trustees.

In other walks of life over 27 years the Trustees have pursued widely differing interests. They have been judges, lawyers, accountants, business people, winemakers, city councillors and aldermen, bureaucrats, administrators and practitioners and patrons of the arts.

When they meet together in the John Bishop Room under the life-size bust of the founder of the Adelaide Festival, they share a common aim: to ensure the best interests of the Festival Centre are served at all times. In turn the Centre must serve the people of South Australia and its cultural life.

Dame Ruby Litchfield and Judge David Bright share the record as the longest-serving Trustees, each with 12 years. Dame Ruby sat on the Trust from 1971 to 1982, and Judge Bright from 1971 to 1980 and 1989 to 1990. Next is lawyer David Quick, with 11 years from 1984 to 1994.

For *By Popular Demand*, six Trustees were chosen by Festival Centre staff, former staff and arts administrators as representing the outstanding dedication and service of the Trust to the Adelaide Festival Centre.

Each of the Trustees was asked to name their most favourite memory of the Festival Centre, visual art or performance.

John Baily, Chair from 1971 to 1975.

"Pedantic. Even more pedantic than me. And he absolutely understood the relationship between the Trust and its chief executive officer, because he ran the Art Gallery. I couldn't have asked for anybody better to help me get the Centre going." – Anthony Steel.

"It was one of the best things I was ever asked to do." – John Baily.

FAVOURITE: The Bert Flugelman environmental sculpture on the south-eastern Plaza – "an entirely satisfying commission for the site".

Australian made

The Trustees have a drinks cabinet in their private box at the Festival Theatre. In the early days the cabinet's original hinges jammed regularly at 45 degrees. Technical manager Dennis Smith replaced them with the struts from the rear door of an EH Holden station wagon. The drinks cabinet has worked perfectly ever since.

Right: Bert Flugelman and his "entirely satisfying commission for the site".

Below: *Because You Are Mine*

Middle: Julie Holledge

Bottom: Dame Ruby Litchfield

Dr Julie Holledge, 1990 to 1995

"I took pleasure in my role as a sounding board. I enjoyed our discussions about the cultural balance of the Centre's programs and the development of mechanisms that allowed us to analyse their effect. We sought to reflect the cultural make-up of the State within those programs. As an arts educator and practitioner I hadn't been involved in the business side of an institution of this size and importance. I learnt a lot."

FAVOURITE: The local Brave New Works program from 1992, including the Red Shed's *Because You Are Mine* by Daniel Keene.

Dame Ruby Litchfield, 1971 to 1983

"Ruby filled every taxi driver in Adelaide with propaganda about the Festival Theatre. It was our baby. We were extremely close to it, and Ruby was closest." – Judge David Bright, fellow first Trustee.

"When I started there were masses of diagrams at the meetings in the Art Gallery. I knew nothing about them. We all had to learn fast. I used to walk through the building and feel I was part of it, and it was part of me. I still feel the Festival Theatre is part of me." – Dame Ruby Litchfield.

FAVOURITE: The 1986 Adelaide Festival.

The late Andrew Noblett, chair from 1984 to 1988

"He was an excellent chair. Andrew had good management skills, was an imaginative thinker and was ambitious for the Centre. He was a really good operator. Many people were very sad when he died of an asthma attack." – Len Amadio.

"Andrew's interest in the Centre was intense – so intense that he told me if I hadn't been appointed general manager he would've put up his hand for the job. His brief was to help change the direction of the Centre, and he did that. He was closely involved in the negotiations for *Cats*, cared about the arts, the commercial direction of the Centre and its relevance to the theatre-going audience of Adelaide." – Tim McFarlane.

FAVOURITE: *Cats*. (Courtesy of Tim McFarlane).

David Quick, 1984 to 1994

"As a lawyer, and particularly as a barrister, I deal with mistaken occurrences. I don't do anything productive except settle disputes. On the Trust I could be part of the production of a great number of events and I could assist people to develop their artistic capacities. I also had the pleasure of the company of the board, the Centre staff and the artists themselves. I enjoyed my time immensely." – David Quick.

FAVOURITE: *Guys and Dolls*.

The late David Wynn, 1975, chair from 1976 to 1980

"The depth of his involvement and the level of support he gave to arts activity in the building was unequalled. David never lost sight of what the building was really there for. In particular he understood the relationship between the Festival and the Festival Centre, and he worked hard to maintain it." – Rob Brookman.

FAVOURITE: State Opera's *The Fiery Angel* at the 1988 Adelaide Festival. (Courtesy of Mrs Patricia Wynn).

Top: Andrew Noblett

Middle: David Quick

Bottom: David Wynn

CHAPTER 22

"We knew we were building something big"

By the time the first sod was turned in Elder Park in March 1970, the theory was that the Festival Hall would need only a dozen people to run it.

There was no hope of that. Long before the opening night in June 1973, the theory had been abandoned. The Festival Hall concept had become a multi-purpose Festival Theatre, then a full-tilt performing arts centre.

The earliest Festival Centre Trust employees were technical manager Dennis Smith, general manager Anthony Steel, deputy general manager Peter Nicholson, accountant Kevin Earle, front-of-house manager George Pullen, box office manager Patti Bennett, publicity manager Tony Frewin, maintenance supervisor Tom Sheils, switchboard operator Marisa Mignone, receptionist Kay Pender and filing clerk Karenza Harrold.

The team operated out of Goldsborough House on North Terrace. Marisa Mignone, on the switchboard, had the whole second floor to herself.

In the beginning the ranks were thin and the work was hard, but the exhilaration was constant. "The hours were long and we didn't worry about it," says Josephine Landsberg, Steel's assistant for four years. "We were never told how to do anything. We had to find out for ourselves.

"It was a time of great trust and integrity in the arts. The whole staff was so excited about the opening of the Festival Theatre and the first Festival in it that everyone helped everyone else. We worked for each other and we worked for the Centre.

"We knew we were building something big."

Today the Centre has 160 full-time staff and 160 casuals, working in 16 departments. Twenty-eight of those staff have been with the Trust for 20 years or more. Many more than that number have moved on to positions of influence as performers, directors, producers, technicians and managers in the arts and entertainment industries around Australia.

Teena Munn, once a secretary to the Festival and now program manager for the Sydney Olympic Arts Festival, noticed the difference when she left Adelaide. "When I went to Sydney I presumed everyone there would know more about the business than we did in Adelaide," she says.

"That wasn't the case at all. We knew more than they did. We didn't realise how well trained we were at the Centre, and how much we learnt. I look back and think they were the hardest times, and the best times. The number of talented people that have come out of the building is amazing."

Here are some of them:

Tim McFarlane and John Robertson are senior executives of the Really Useful Company and the Cameron Mackintosh organisation respectively. Rob Brookman

Left: Shane Mountifield, Denise Lovick, Heather Blewett, Marisa Mignone, Angelo Mitsoulis, Laraine Wheeler

runs Arts Projects Australia. Penny Chapman is a former head of drama for ABC TV. Mary Vallentine is general manager of the Sydney Symphony Orchestra.

Geoffrey Rush, Academy Award winner, spent a vital part of his acting career with State Theatre Company's Lighthouse at the Playhouse. Neil Armfield was one of his directors there. Director Gale Edwards, much in demand for big musicals and a favourite of Andrew Lloyd Webber, had her start with *The Labours of Hercules* at Come Out '83.

The playwright Nick Enright's career first flourished with STC. Michael Siberry is a senior ensemble actor with the Royal Shakespeare Company.

Ghillian Sullivan, a principal soprano with Opera Australia, had her first professional role as the Plaintiff in Gilbert and Sullivan's *Trial by Jury* in an early Festival Centre production in 1976.

Mort Clark has his own production company in Sydney. Chris Potter is head mechanist with Opera Australia. Alan Knox was lighting master with the Queensland Performing Arts Trust and is now a freelance production manager working for the Brisbane Festival.

And then there are those who stayed or returned. The Festival Centre has a deserved reputation for professionalism front-of-house, backstage and in administration. Six long-standing employees try to explain why. Most of it comes back to the magic of theatre:

Heather Blewett, stage door attendant and backstage photographer to the stars

"I fell in love with the theatre when I worked for 10 years as an usher. Then when I moved to the stage door I felt so much more a part of the show. The surprising thing about the big stars is that the bigger they are the nicer they are. I have my favourites – Nancye Hayes, the late Ricky May, Toni Lamond, Cameron Daddo, Simon Gallaher, Jeannie Little, Bert Newton, Billy Connolly, Hayley Mills, Sir John Mills. The list goes on."

FAVOURITE: Peter Allen concert.

Denise Lovick, casual lighting technician, now production manager

"The challenge of this life is meeting the production deadline and working with such diverse people and personalities. When I was young I used to like the magic of the theatre. Now I know what the magic is and I still like it."

FAVOURITE: *Barnum.*

Marisa Mignone, original employee, now deputy theatre services manager

"We witness the best performances off-stage here, some good, some bad, others astonishing, and what the audience sees is a tiny part of reality. Then there are the audiences themselves, which range from agreeable and pleasant to extraordinary and outrageous. People often say this is not the real world. I think it is."

FAVOURITE: *Les Miserables.*

Angelo Mitsoulis, cleaner for 22 years

"As a printer I watched machinery for 25 years, so it was a pleasure to come to the Festival Centre and have the opportunity to see and talk to so many international stars like Liza Minnelli. And I get a kick out of the actors who remember the staff. Geoffrey Rush, John Wood and Gary Sweet always say 'hello'. I only hope cost-cutting doesn't affect what the Centre does too much. I miss the Christmas shows, and so do the patrons."

FAVOURITE: *Cats.*

Shane Mountifield, building services manager

"Working in the building industry within the arts industry is a unique experience on a daily basis for our team, as is being involved with an icon of the State. We have different challenges all the time, working around the shows. The camaraderie at the Centre is great. I'm amazed by the number of characters who drift in and out of the place, and I'm equally amazed by the number of characters who stay. The Trust encourages its staff to take up new challenges. Mine is to introduce some sparkle to the refurbishment, so the Festival Centre is the star at the top of the tree, where it belongs."

FAVOURITE: Annual staff fancy-dress boat race on the River Torrens.

Laraine Wheeler, stage manager of the Trust's first production, *Winnie the Pooh,* in 1973, now Playhouse lighting operator

"Most people wait until the weekend to have a good time. That's when we work hardest and have the best time. We do the same things but differently every time, with a huge number of talented people. After all these years it's still a buzz to witness extraordinary performances."

FAVOURITE: *Guys and Dolls.*

Organ donor

The Festival Centre's Silver Jubilee Organ is the world's only musical hovercraft. It floats to and from the Festival Theatre stage and its home in the wings on a cushion of air. The organ has 4250 pipes and was built by the Austrian firm Rieger Orgelbau. The public of South Australia donated most of its $430,000 cost. The organ's grand opening concert on 4 April 1979 featured soloists Peter Hurford and Ashleigh Tobin, with the Adelaide Symphony Orchestra conducted by Elyakum Shapirra. But there may have been another musical force at work that night. Among the donors acknowledged in the concert souvenir program is Elvis Presley. The King's Adelaide fans made an In Memoriam gift, and Elvis was last heard playing *Edge of Reality* on the Festival Centre's Silver Jubilee Organ in the early hours of 16 August 1997.

CHAPTER 23

The Centre of John Bishop's Festival

Professor John Bishop started the Adelaide Festival of Arts in 1960, with a little help from his friends in the Adelaide Establishment. A festival based on the model of the Edinburgh Festival was first proposed at a meeting at the Adelaide Town Hall in 1958.

Professor Bishop chaired the meeting. He became the Festival's first artistic director, its driving force. He died in London in 1964 while on Festival business, but not before the campaign to find a home for the Festival had begun to gather momentum.

Without John Bishop there wouldn't be a Festival Centre today, and the John Bishop Room in the Centre acknowledges the founder's great contribution to the cultural life of South Australia. The decisions that affect the Festival, the Centre, and their relationship are made by both bodies' boards in the "JB Room".

Those decisions haven't always been mutually acceptable, or the relationship always smooth, and the Festival doesn't live in the Festival Centre any more. In 1996 its administration moved to the more comfortable Norwich House in North Adelaide, finally giving in to the centre's chronic office accommodation squeeze after Christopher Hunt's troubled Festival in 1994.

That year the State Government was so horrified with the Festival's financial state that it considered ordering the Festival Board of Governors to pay the outstanding costs, or make the Board vote itself out of existence. The Government opted for a new Board which now acts for the Minister for the Arts, Diana Laidlaw.

From 1980 until then, the general manager of the Festival Centre Trust was also general manager of the Festival. Mostly it was an harmonious arrangement; the Festival was housed by the Festival Centre Trust, which made all its resources available for the event itself.

The late Andrew Noblett, the Trust's chair during the mid-1980s, believed the single most important project of the Trust was total support for the Festival.

John Bishop – without him there wouldn't be a Festival Centre

While not standard practice, the Trust, as host organisation, occasionally has absorbed substantial Festival expenses by waiving theatre rentals and other costs. It may or may not surprise Government Arts Ministers over the years that the books of more than one Festival were balanced between the office of the Trust general manager of the day and the John Bishop Room.

As recently as 1996 the Trust helped reduce the deficit of that year's Festival.

The distancing of the relationship between the Festival and the Festival Centre Trust concerns many people who were paid by the Trust and willingly worked for the Festival when required. Tim McFarlane, former general manager of both, describes the separation of the two organisations "as a great shame, a great waste".

Since Robyn Archer's 1998 Festival, a degree of unity has been restored. The Festival still uses the resources of an entire cultural complex to present the premier arts festival in Australia, and one of the most important in the world.

Yet an Adelaide Festival Centre without an Adelaide Festival in it would not have been what Professor John Bishop had in mind, and Robyn Archer is conscious of this. "Building the Festival Centre ensured both the future of the Festival and a cultural life all year round for the citizens of Adelaide," she says.

Below: The Squeezebox on the Plaza at the 1998 Festival

Above: 1998 and 2000 Adelaide Festival artistic director Robyn Archer

Right: Opening night of the 1998 Telstra Adelaide Festival, with *Flamma Flamma*

Casino no-no

In 1979, Adelaide's first casino was planned for the Festival Theatre upstairs foyer. It was to run for the three weeks of the 1980 Adelaide Festival, would be managed by Hobart's Wrest Point Casino, and would help pay for director Christopher Hunt's program. Casinos were illegal in South Australia at the time, so the idea never made it to the bank.

"It's obvious that a great deal of the success of the Festival over the years can be attributed to this highly workable and accommodating space. With the revitalisation of the West End, this precinct will become an even more powerful urban cultural statement. I have no doubt that a healthy future for the Adelaide Festival depends very much on how the Centre is used and to what extent the two administrations can work harmoniously for the mutual good.

"Future Festival artistic directors will always choose to use the Centre to the max. In the end the effectiveness of those choices will depend on the administrations making productive collaborative decisions to make them work."

CHAPTER 24

"A fantastic eight years"

Like Kevin Earle, Tim McFarlane was an accountant head-hunted from the Adelaide electronic media. He was general manager of the Adelaide Festival Centre Trust from 1986 to 1994. From 1984 he was the Trust's business manager and later deputy general manager. McFarlane's early days were a time of constant drama as the divisive Earle years came to a close.

The Trust, through its chairman Andrew Noblett, demanded a change of direction and style. Too much time was being spent on striking deals for the big musicals, not enough on the business within the Centre and its overall artistic objectives. The State Government, through the Department for the Arts, felt likewise.

In mid-1984 the Trust was on its knees financially. It had to ask the State Government for an advance on the following year's grant. McFarlane unashamedly set about rebuilding the Centre on a commercial basis. He brought in new people and encouraged existing staff to achieve their potential.

"I was completely convinced that through a stable commercial performance the Trust would be able to do more artistically," McFarlane says.

Before he went, Earle taught McFarlane the ropes, including him in negotiations for *Cats* and *Guys and Dolls*. "I got on well with Kevin," McFarlane says. "I respected him for his absolute commitment to the job, and I learnt from him and John Robertson." The experience was to stand him in good stead when the Trust launched its second wave of musicals in 1988 with *My Fair Lady*.

A major turning point came in 1986. *Cats*, Earle's greatest legacy, began to perform at the eastern States box offices. Other business units picked up. "It was not an easy process," McFarlane says. "The change was brought about by a combination of management and artistic decisions with the very active support of the Trustees, who looked critically but constructively at our every move.

"We found a good balance. The commercial musicals attracted hundreds of thousands of people while I was there, and their success allowed us to do a lot of other things. We expanded our education and art programs, commissioned new work, set up the cabaret club in the Space, and developed programs for young people.

"I still believe that while it is not the only thing, the production of musicals is a legitimate part of what the Trust is about."

McFarlane went to Andrew Lloyd Webber's Really Useful Company after a "fantastic eight years. I still miss the Centre at Festival time, but I don't miss running a public sector organisation. I feel extremely liberated in the private sector. However, I have no regrets about having worked for the Trust.

"Arts buildings aren't worth a cracker unless you have wonderful things going on in them. We had some wonderful things at the Festival Centre.

"When I moved away from Adelaide I was able to see the quite remarkable effect the Festival Centre had had on the arts in Australia, in the Dunstan era and then for the decade until a few years ago. Artists, management, marketing, technical positions – the Centre has led the way."

Why?

Below: Tim McFarlane – "We had some wonderful things at the Festival Centre"

Some Enchanted Lunchtime

Tim McFarlane and entrepreneur John Frost agreed on *South Pacific* as a joint venture over lunch at the staid and exclusive Adelaide Club, where McFarlane is a member. McFarlane will not confirm the story that he broke into "Some Enchanted Evening" over the port.

Because, says McFarlane, "the Festival Centre is people, vision and money. For the first two, the Centre needs the third. In this economic climate governments are winding back levels of support for the arts, and the South Australian Government is winding back more than most. It doesn't have the same commitment to the arts as other States, when once South Australia showed the others how.

"Cutbacks in the Trust's budgets for programming projects are frustrating the Centre's people with vision. In my time there I was frustrated that there was never enough money to maintain the buildings. Now there is some money for that, but it's irrelevant if things aren't happening inside the buildings.

"The Centre must not retreat purely into a venue management role, or a place for speech nights and annual general meetings. That would be so sad and unnecessary, because I passionately believe in what the Festival Centre has stood for and should stand for, and I always will."

Tim McFarlane's affection and concern for the Festival Centre is appreciated by the Trust's new chief executive officer Kate Brennan.

"Going backwards is the last thing on our minds at the Centre," she says. "We believe passionately too, and retreat is not the action of passionate people.

"The Festival Centre is moving forward with renewed vision into the next century."

Day and night for 100 years

The Festival Theatre "cost about a tenth of what the Sydney Opera House did, was built in a tenth of the time, and is ten times more successful as a place for housing performances. It is a place filled day and night with activity, light, sun and welcome; a brilliant piece of design with sudden exhilarating spaces and sights; cheerfully efficient, unpretentious, delicate in its details."

Andrew Porter, the arts correspondent of London's *Financial Times*, wrote those words in 1976. The Adelaide Festival Centre then was young and fresh. It could do no wrong.

In 1998 the Festival Centre is 25 years old. The concerns expressed by former Trust general manager Tim McFarlane in the previous chapter are shared by many who care about the place once "filled day and night with activity".

Times are changing, and so the Festival Centre is changing with them.

The era of the big blockbuster musical, in which the Festival Centre Trust played a leading role and prospered accordingly, is perhaps drawing to a close. *The King and I* cost $2 million to mount in Adelaide. By the time it reached Broadway it cost $6 million. The trend may be to smaller musicals – a cast of six for $1 million, instead of a cast of 30 for $5 million.

In 1973 home entertainment was television, hi-fi, radio, playing cards and board games. In 1998 it is computers, video games, giant screens, total leisure centres in the lounge room.

When people look beyond the house for diversions, they turn increasingly to bigger event-based entertainments such as the Adelaide Festival, WOMADELAIDE, "operas in the outback" and large concerts. They see their dollars going further that way. The Centre also feels the competition from the city's restaurant culture, and the pokies.

In turn the Government dollars are going less far. In 1973 State Government funding made up between 60 and 70 per cent of the Centre's income. Today it is 11 per cent. Government support for the Centre for the 1997/98 financial year

Above: Former Trust chief executive
Bill Cossey

Above: Festival Centre Trust chief
executive Kate Brennan

is a million dollars less than it was six years ago. Any more shrinkage and the Centre will shrink – in its services, its programs and its productions.

So too will its sphere of influence within the world of arts and entertainment.

The Festival Centre still works fine. Adelaide Festival artistic director Robyn Archer can vouch for that: "I've performed in almost every imaginable space there – Theatre, Playhouse, Space, Amphitheatre, lawns, foyers, galleries, Plaza, the lot. And I know as an artist who's played all over Australia and in many places in the world that the Festival Centre is one of the most workable multi-space complexes anywhere.

"It certainly needs a make-over, mainly technically, but its stages remain incredibly popular with artists. Many high-profile visiting artists and companies claim their work has never looked as good as it does in the Festival Centre.

"The foyers are useable because they're audience-friendly and at last in the 1998 Festival the Plaza came alive too, with the Squeezebox, and a young audience inhabited the space, using it and enjoying it. It was one of my aims, and we got there."

So no visiting theatre, opera or dance company or international entrepreneur would knock back the Festival Centre as a venue for their shows. Its youth and public access programs such as Something on Saturday and Sunday Salon are going strong. Theatre, dance and music still pull a crowd.

To meet the challenges of the future, the Trust has a five-year master plan. A $3.6 million refurbishment of the Festival Theatre and its foyers will be followed by a State Government-backed environmental enhancement plan which will create stronger connections and improve access between the facilities, the Torrens, the Plaza and the public.

The Centre must develop physically to maintain its status in the arts and the wider communities of Adelaide, South Australia and Australia. It has to become more accessible so it maintains its competitive position in the marketplace. Former Trust chief executive officer Bill Cossey reasons that linking the Centre with other city attractions would create a "bustling, thriving precinct with enough appeal for people simply to wander around and enjoy the ambience".

He also believes the Centre needs a daytime weekday focus.

The live arts are the most dynamic form of entertainment. The Trust believes those arts will never die. The special feeling of sharing with the audience implicit in live performance has sustained the live arts for thousands of years.

The Festival Centre will continue to be a place of that special sharing, provided it goes with the tide of change. "The Festival Centre has always been at the forefront of the performing arts in Australia," says Trust chief executive officer Kate Brennan. "It has never been an anachronism, and it is our job to ensure that it never will be.

"The Centre's 25th birthday is the right time to reaffirm those goals of commitment to the stimulation of people culturally and intellectually, to entertaining them across a broad range, to introducing young people to the arts, to encouraging artists. We are looking not only to the second 25 years. We are looking to the first 100 years.

"The people of South Australia have a great affection for the Festival Centre. They're very proud of it, even if they have never set foot inside the door. And those who do come through the doors have a great time. There will be many more great times.

"The history of the Festival Centre doesn't suit a theatre for hire, and I didn't come to it to run a facility alone. I came here to manage a creative organisation. The world is changing very quickly and we have to change with it. More than that, we have to be ahead of the change, ahead of the game.

"The Festival Centre has been the epitome of energy before, and it will be again. This place has an exciting destiny. On behalf of all South Australians we will make the Festival Centre sing again."

And dance and act and laugh and cry and imagine all manner of things, day and night for a hundred years.

First principles

The Festival Centre is built on Kaurna land, where for tens of thousands of years Australia's Aboriginal people held festivals of their own by other names. They chose the site for much the same reason as Steele Hall did – by the water, on a gentle slope, an abundance of trees. It was a place of natural beauty and it was the Kaurna people's home. Indigenous companies such as Bangarra Dance Theatre and Black Swan Theatre have performed at the Festival Centre and Aboriginal artists have exhibited there. Aboriginal stories have been told there. The Festival Centre is conscious of both its link and its debt to the Kaurna people of South Australia, and in its 25th year in 1998 presented the exhibition *Spirit of Place: Black Land White Shells – 3 Views of Kaurna Territory*, by Aboriginal artists Nicole Cumpston, Agnes Love and Darren Siwes.

Left: Tanendi, 1998 by Nicole Cumpston

Flowers power

*Shopping and F***ing* in 1997 was not the Festival Centre's first R-rated stage show. The honour belongs to Lindsay Kemp's *Flowers*, right, at the Playhouse in July 1976. The Centre's publicity manager Tony Frewin had a field day. "For the first time we will turn away people under 18," he said. "The show features nudity and almost every form of human sexuality and savagery," and moral-protection groups reacted accordingly. Court action was threatened, and on the sell-out opening night the Festival of Light and the Christian Revival Crusade, lower right, demonstrated outside the theatre. After the show Festival of Light chairman Dr David Phillips admitted *Flowers* was highly symbolic and could be interpreted in different ways by different individuals. However, he added "if these things were done in Rundle Street a bloke would be arrested". *Flowers* played to packed houses for its 25 performances and during the run Kemp and company put on matinees of *Mr Punch's Pantomime* for children.

Edifice complex

The film star Richard Harris, left, took the old Excalibur to Adelaide arts writers during the touring season of the musical *Camelot* in November 1984. As well as playing King Arthur, Harris twice invited full houses at the Festival Theatre to stay behind and hear his views on Adelaide *Advertiser* articles about the show by the author of this book and journalist Christobel Botten. Harris sat on a stool centre-stage waving clippings of the stories he called "irresponsible" and "rubbish" and a "slur". He said: "I am not doing this in defence of myself, but indeed in defence of the theatre itself . . . This for us here is a sort of sacred monument. It is like a chapel to us here and we treat it as such." The post-encore outbursts made front-page news around Australia. Ms Botten observed later that Richard Harris had been "perfectly polite to me" during research for her backstage feature article, and she had not been "terribly rude" in her writing. "If I had wanted to be bitchy I had all the material in the world."

Production Credits —

Project co-ordinator Kate Jordan-Moore, Andrew Bleby, Kate Brennan, Rob Brookman, Bill Cossey

Len Amadio, Robyn Archer, Basil Arty, John Baily, Peter Barnes, Patti Bennett, Heather Blewett, Tessa Bremner, David Bright, Ciro Cantone, Wally Carr, Ann Churchill-Brown, Sonia Coorey, Tony Cox, Shirley Stott Despoja, Tony Dawson, Lauren Drewery, Lorraine Douglas, Don Dunstan, Peter Farrell, Rodney Fisher, Fred Flood, Joyce Forbes, Maxine Forrester, Bev George, John Glennon, Peter Goers, Rosemary Gordon, Andy Hall, Steele Hall, Silver Harris, Bruce Harry, Colin Hassell, Noni Hazlehurst, Nicholas Heyward, Lorna Hurford, Rainer Jozeps, Ruby Litchfield, Reg Livermore, Josephine Landsberg, Denise Lovick, Tim McFarlane, John Mignone, Marisa Mignone, Hayley Mills, Karmen Moore, John Morphett, Teena Munn, Lesley Newton, Jon Nicholls, Ann Peters, Sharon Polkinghorne and the staff of *The Advertiser* Library, Marie Powers, Mike Pryce, John Robertson, Geoffrey Rush, Michael Scheid, David Sly, Dennis Smith, Anthony Steel, Vivonne Thwaites, Peter Ward, Laraine Wheeler, Gough Whitlam, Ken Wilby, David Wilson, Ron Wood, Patricia Wynn and everyone else who pointed us in yet another of the Adelaide Festival Centre's thousand and one directions.

Zac and Ceefa; Tim, Kate, Lucy and Alice.

Most of all, Jo Peoples and the Performing Arts Collection of South Australia.

Sources —

Adelaide Festival Theatre: Report on Overseas Visit, by F. C. Hassell, 1969; *The Advertiser; The Australian; Festival! The Story of the Adelaide Festival of Arts*, by Derek Whitelock, 1980; *A Feasibility Study for the Adelaide Festival Hall*, by Thomas DeGaetani, 1968; *A Guide to Public Art works – Adelaide Festival Centre and environs*, by John Neylon and Margot Osborne, 1993; Mortlock Library of South Australia; *The News*; recorded interviews with Festival Centre staff and Len Amadio by Jo Peoples and Peter Goers; Restless Films; *A Singular Act – Twenty Five Years of the State Theatre Company of South Australia*, by Peter Ward, 1992; *The Sunday Mail*; Opera Australia Archives.

Again, JOPAC.